THE MINDFULNESS PLAYBOOK

Dr BARBARA MARIPOSA

First published in Great Britain in 2016 by Hodder & Stoughton.
An Hachette UK company.

This edition published in 2017 by John Murray Learning

Hardback ISBN: 978 147 3 63619 4

Paperback ISBN: 978 147 3 63620 0

eBook ISBN: 978 147 3 63621 7

1

Designed and set by Craig Burgess.

Printed and bound in Great Britain by CPI Group (UK) Ltd, Croydon, CR0 4YY.

John Murray Learning policy is to use papers that are natural, renewable and recyclable products and made from wood grown in sustainable forests. The logging and manufacturing processes are expected to conform to the environmental regulations of the country of origin.

John Murray Learning
Carmelite House
50 Victoria Embankment
London EC4Y 0DZ

www.hodder.co.uk

Also available
as an ebook

• • • • • •
CONTENTS

Trained at the Royal Free Hospital, London, Dr Barbara worked in psychiatry and public health. While at medical school, she obtained a B.Sc. in psychology and began a life-long enquiry into the interdependence of mental, emotional and physical wellbeing.

Bringing together her extensive knowledge, training skills and experience in meditation, Dr Barbara created the powerful and pioneering Mind Mood Mastery programme on which this book and her corporate work is based.

Her passion is to create the kind of leadership and organisational culture that supports mental and emotional wellbeing, and to break down the stigma and prejudice around mental illness. Her vision: healthy energised people powering exceptional business performance.

She co-authored *The Kindness Habit: Transforming our Relationship to Addictive Behaviours* and *Leading with Presence: What is it, Why it Matters and How to Get it*. The latter brings together mindfulness and emotional intelligence in a simple science-based model, the Presence Pyramid.

In her one-to-one work, Dr Barbara supports people, at whatever stage in their life they may be, to make the most of their natural abilities and energy, to be happy, healthy and fulfilled.

She is an accomplished public speaker, bringing simplicity, originality and honesty to her presentations and drawing on her own journey through mental illness into full wellbeing, profound personal experiences that inform all the work she does.

······

INTRODUCTION

••••••

The way it is

What you hold in your hands right now is a no-nonsense, informative book that breaks the rules. I invite you to write in it, scribble in it, draw in it and generally make the book your own document of learning and creativity. It also has the potential to turn your life around.

By engaging with the content of this book, you will learn unique tools and skills that can bring you greater energy, freedom and clarity.

When we are fully present, a certain kind of spaciousness arises, an aliveness that is not tied to the outer circumstances of our life, a sense of being anchored in ourselves that allows us to ride the waves of life on a surfboard of our own making. This book gives you some ideas about how to make that surfboard and keep upgrading it.

It may seem paradoxical but, if you want to live life with a sense of energy, enjoyment and adventure, a good place to start is to master stillness. In stillness, we come to see our thoughts and feelings as passing events: coming and going like the weather, with whatever weight and significance we choose to give them. We get in touch with a deeper awareness of who we are, whole, complete and able.

......

'IT'S NOT THE MECHANICAL ACT OF HITTING THE BALL; IT'S WHAT'S GOING ON IN YOUR HEAD THAT DETERMINES WHETHER YOU WIN OR LOSE.'

......

Roger Federer

As you start to embed new habits that have a positive impact on your resilience, adaptability and energy management, you might start to wonder why you weren't taught this stuff in school.

We'll explore ways to create **Mindful Moments** – short breathing spaces where you can land, connect and recharge, and then spring off from again. There are six **Power Tools** – ways to get yourself out of tricky situations and back in touch with the effective clear-headed you. We will also develop the **Daily Formal Practice** of meditating in a mindful way every day, and discover the **Six Competencies of Emotional Intelligence** (EQ).

'BY ENGAGING WITH
THE CONTENT OF
THIS BOOK, YOU WILL
LEARN UNIQUE TOOLS
AND SKILLS THAT CAN
BRING YOU GREATER
ENERGY, FREEDOM
AND CLARITY.'

The age of endarkenment

Somewhere along the line, with the dawning of what in the Western world is ironically called the Age of Enlightenment, we all got very dark, serious and mysterious about what was wrong with us and why. 'What's wrong with me? Why? I'm hurting therefore I must be broken. I need fixing.'

The approach in this book leans in another direction: 'How can I make the best of the talents and abilities I have? How can I best contribute these to the world? How can I embrace the challenges and difficulties that being human inevitably brings in such a way that I learn, grow and become wiser? How can I realize the potential of my pain rather than anaesthetize it, deny it or medicalize it?'

The way out

The content of this book – based on the 'Mind Mood Mastery' (MMM) courses I've been running since 2013 – is a bit like a three-stranded rope, weaving together mindfulness, emotional intelligence and wellbeing psychology.

The content has been road tested for three things:

1. **Practical applicability** – useful, relevant and doable.
2. **Efficacy** – it works.
3. **Scientific validity** – there's evidence that it works.

If you will allow me to carry the metaphor a step farther, this rope can be seen as a direct line of access to a place of renewable energy and power within yourself.

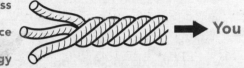

Imagine a lake. People are throwing pebbles into the lake so its surface is covered in spreading circles of ripples, colliding into one other, causing interference patterns. This is what the average mind is like, full of wandering thoughts and random associations, reacting with new ripples every time something happens, someone says something, or some life event throws a new pebble into the pond. Sometimes it's more like a gigantic boulder than a pebble.

The mud on the bottom of the lake gets churned up. There's a background hum of some emotional quality that you can't quite identify. You feel vaguely perturbed,

stressed and anxious, and you are not really sure why.
This has become your 'normal'.

Now imagine the surface of the lake stilling, clearing,
calming, so you can see right down to the bottom.
The mud has settled and there is clarity. Maybe a
new pebble gives rise to a ripple. A single ripple is
manageable. We can see it, notice the effect, and allow
the mud to settle and the ripple to pass. This clarity of
awareness is achievable.

Life is not a spectator sport. Buying sneakers and all the kit
doesn't make you fit enough to run a marathon. We have to
actually *do* the things that enable us to *be* in better shape
mentally, emotionally and physically.

······

'IMPATIENCE ASKS FOR THE IMPOSSIBLE AND
WANTS TO REACH ITS GOAL WITHOUT THE
MEANS OF GETTING THERE.'

······

G. W. F. Hegel

And ... it's much easier than you may have been led to
believe. We can get the 'ripples' or waves, generated by the
systems of our body and mind, to be in sync with each

other. As any physicist will tell you, when waves are in sync, their power is amplified. Within human systems this translates as greater energy, clarity and focus – what is called **coherence**.

One of the easiest and quickest ways to create coherence, and be more focused, balanced and clear headed, is to slow down and deepen your breathing.

> *Try it now.* Feel your feet on the ground. Release your shoulders and jaw a little. Focus your attention on your chest area. Take a deep breath in and exhale slowly. Do this twice more. Notice how you feel. Try it again throughout your day today. The effects are cumulative.

Now try this thought on for size: 'I am not my thoughts; I *have* thoughts.'

Most of us, most of the time, live lost in thought, literally. We are not present, we are lost in the constant chatter of thought, identifying with it and listening to it as though it were a true and accurate representation of reality.

I call my internal chatter 'Radio Barbara'. It's like an old friend. I know it well. Radio Barbara has a habit of telling me 'I can't, shouldn't, shouldn't have, need to, mustn't, ought to – you idiot!' My radio station has a strongly self-critical bent. It's like a band of chattering monkeys.

Step back for a moment right now and notice what

thoughts are passing through your mind. Yes, those ones. Be still and listen. Write in this box what you hear, what your inner chatter is, what your chattering monkeys are saying.

> **WHAT THOUGHTS ARE YOU HAVING RIGHT NOW?**
> e.g. 'I'm not having any thoughts.' That is a thought right there.

Why bother?

Learning how to make the best use of our innate mental and emotional capacities is the next big thing on the public health agenda. It has to be. Stress, anxiety, exhaustion, burnout, addictions and depression already take a terrible toll. They are predicted by the World Health Organization (WHO) to be the second biggest causes of ill health in First World countries by 2020.

It is estimated that the costs of this invisible, silent epidemic will soon be greater than that of treating cancer, diabetes and lung disease combined. Despite our wealth and material affluence, we are not any happier than we were decades ago.

We are all in it together. We all suffer in our inner lives. Society's current construction of mental suffering as being negative influences how 'I', the individual, engage with and relate to it within myself. I sincerely hope that this book will, first, give people the means to achieve greater 'whole person' wellness, and, second, create a more open, accepting and compassionate conversation around mental and emotional unwellness.

......

'MATERIAL WEALTH WITHOUT INNER PEACE
IS LIKE DYING OF THIRST WHILE
SWIMMING IN A LAKE.'

......

Paramhansa Yogananda

My personal commitment is to give as many people as possible the tools and skills to make that WHO prediction wrong.

What's possible?

This book enables you to make the most of three characteristics that set human beings apart from other mammals, characteristics that we are all born with – namely,

- our ability for self-reflection.
- our emotional intelligence.
- our potential for continuing personal growth.

The cultural construct of the human life trajectory reflects an underlying assumption that growth and learning slow down and stop as life proceeds along its linear path. That the brain and other organs of the body, once we stop growing physically, just deteriorate. That we shrink as we get older, not just physically but metaphysically. Think of the road sign that is used to represent older people.

This is not how it is. This is how it is:

Older		Wisdom
and	=	Wellbeing
Growing		Wonderful relationships

Science itself is now proving this, and, since we live in an era that values science so highly, people are starting to listen. Millions of people are taking up practices hitherto seen as whacky, fringe or silly because science is proving not just *that* they work but also *how* they work.

. . . . . .

REGARDLESS OF
AGE, PAST STORY
OR PRESENT
CIRCUMSTANCES, FROM
WHEREVER WE ARE,
RIGHT HERE, RIGHT
NOW, WE CAN MOVE
FORWARD AND GROW.

. . . . . .

The science bit

NEUROPLASTICITY

The brain changes shape according to how you use it. That 1.25-kilo lump of tofu-like tissue inside your skull is a self-organizing, highly adaptive living system of untold power. The instruction manual most of us have been given, however, is sadly lacking. Maybe that's why so many people are turning to the ancient wisdom traditions, where the understanding of and instruction manuals for the human mind and human suffering are far more comprehensive and compassionate.

The ability for the brain to change, adapt and mould itself according to use is called neuroplasticity. The way your brain is structured and functions now is the result of how you've been using it to date. It's been shifting and reshaping all your life as a result of the experiences you've had and what you've made of them.

The continual creation of new nerve cells – **neurogenesis** – is the norm. When I was at medical school in the 1970s we were taught that you were born with a certain number of nerve cells in the brain and that they died progressively as we got older. That was it. There was no new growth. This clearly fed into popular view of ageing as a downhill slide. In recent years, the opposite has been shown to be true.

THE HEART'S BRAIN

There are nerve cells in the heart like the ones in the brain. There are also cells that secrete important chemicals such as oxytocin and other neuropeptides, previously thought to come only from the brain. Your heart has its own brain.

Sometimes the heart's nerve cells respond faster than the ones in your brain. The heart sends messages to the brain before the brain is aware of experiencing things and interpreting them. That's why your intuition arises so quickly. Often, your head then steps in and rationalizes away your instinctive feeling.

How often have you had an intuition about something but have talked yourself out of it and later discovered that your intuition was right? Your head won over your heart because we live in an age where rationality, knowledge and analytical thought are valued more highly than emotional responses and intuitive wisdom. That situation is changing.

THE BODY'S TRUTH

Your body sends messages to your brain that affect how the brain works. It's not just a top–down brain to body affair. Information about posture, facial expression and patterns of movement have a profound effect not only on our emotional state but also on our cognitive abilities.

Artists create ways to capture and express the essence of the human experience in ways that words never can. Works of art, be they music, painting, theatre, sculpture or the written word, evoke a visceral response in us.

Have you ever been upset about something and not been able to find words to express yourself? When we are upset, key areas of the brain to do with speech go offline. We can't find words because these areas of the brain are not plugged in.

Trauma experts recognize the limitations of talking, analysing, understanding and answering the question 'Why?' in helping us to be free from unpleasant associations or past conditioning. Many are turning to embodied techniques to help people realize their healing potential. The body is a powerful vehicle of self-expression and point of entry for releasing past hurts.

......

'NEUROSCIENCE SHOWS US THAT THE ONLY WAY THAT WE CAN CHANGE THE WAY WE FEEL IS BY BEING AWARE OF OUR INNER EXPERIENCE AND LEARNING TO BEFRIEND WHAT IS GOING ON INSIDE OURSELVES.'

......

Bessel van der Kolk

The age of wisdom revisited

Self-awareness has been around for between 100,000 and 150,000 years. We see evidence for abstract thinking and self-reflection in cave paintings. Our ability to reflect on our own behaviour and existence is due to the development of certain parts of the brain that most other mammals don't seem to have. (I'm treading carefully here – India has granted dolphins non-human personhood.)

It seems that being able to show up, here, now, has been a bit of a puzzle to humankind for a *very long time*. About 2,000 years ago, the Roman Stoic philosopher Seneca wrote: 'When shall we live if not now?' Well, exactly. However, he committed suicide after being accused of plotting the downfall of the Emperor Nero, the one said to have fiddled while Rome burned. Not much evidence of being present there!

And that's the thing, isn't it? When else can we live if not now? The future is, as Joe Strummer said, 'unwritten' ... and the past? Well, it's gone, except in our memory and even that is not accurate. Every time you retrieve a memory it alters slightly. All there is is the present.

In 1971 Ram Dass, a former research faculty member at Harvard and previously named Richard Alpert, became famous for publishing a book called *Be Here Now*. He fell out with his colleagues around the use of hallucinogenics and got fired. But the title of his book still holds up.

In the twenty-first century, after 300 years of unrivalled

and unquestioned supremacy, the brain inside our skulls – and, by inference, the rational mind – is being toppled from its top-dog position. The physical and emotional parts of being human are being scientifically shown to have equal, if not greater, importance.

Emotional intelligence (EQ) correlates more highly than IQ with career success. Leaders need to show integrity, empathy and innovation, all qualities that have far more to do with soft skills than intellect. Global connectivity demands that we are better at connecting emotionally to ourselves, others and the bigger picture. EQ depends on being embodied – aware and in tune with how we feel.

Perhaps the ancient wisdom traditions that suggested mind, body and emotion were all part of one energetic system are right. In which case, the question becomes how we can best manage, maintain and maximize our most precious resource – *human energy*.

Health warning

The practices in this book come with a health warning. There is a risk that, by following the contents in this book, even 10 per cent of it, you could feel better about yourself, your life and the people in it. It's a bit like Pilates. You're building a strong inner core. Your overall wellbeing might improve, and you might feel more at ease, more energized and more comfortable in your own skin.

The permanence paradox

As a child of seven or eight, I remember lying face down on a bridge, peering between its planks at the water below, pondering the nature of the river and its ripples. Try as I might, I couldn't pin it down. Every ripple was in constant motion and yet seemed to stay the same. The river was always there, but the water was flowing forwards all the time. I had no idea that I was pondering the imponderable. I could not possibly have articulated the questions I was seeking to answer, questions about permanence, change and the nature of reality.

Just like Tancredi, a character in Giuseppe Tomasi di Lampedusa's novel, *The Leopard*, I thought that, even as everything changes, so it stays the same. Impermanence is the nature of things and yet the world appears to us stable and unchanging. To accept this paradox is to come to terms with the nature of reality. As we change so we become more ourselves.

This pretty much sums up the journey we go on in choosing to live mindfully. Each moment passes and still we are sitting. Each life event hits us and still we are ourselves. Each challenge we learn from takes us closer to who we have always been.

'But which is the stone that supports the bridge?' Kublai Khan asks.

'The bridge is not supported by one stone or another,' Marco Polo answers, 'but by the line of the arch that they form.'

Kublai Khan remains silent, reflecting. Then he adds: 'Why do you speak to me of the stones? It is only the arch that matters to me.'

Polo answers: 'Without stones there is no arch.'

Italo Calvino, *Invisible Cities*

Enough of the philosophy. Let's get on with it.

The way it works

We are all in different places in our lives and reading this book for different reasons. In my experience, what unites us is a common desire to be at peace within ourselves and make the best of who we are. Some parts of the book will resonate with you more than others. Some may not gel at all on first or even second reading, and that's fine. I invite you to see this book as a roadmap with signposts and take from it what works for you.

Having said that, if you hit a roadblock, there may be some value in exploring further. The mind can be a slippery thing and generate smokescreens to throw us off track. The main thing is to keep up with the Daily Formal Practice, have a sense of curiosity towards the roadblock, and kindness towards yourself.

In Unit 1 we build the foundations. We'll explore how to do the **Daily Formal Practice** and discover some of the science behind what happens in the brain. We'll also introduce the first of the eight **Skill Set for Health** themes. Then there's the first of the 'homework' assignments that accompany each unit.

The other seven Skill Set for Health themes will be introduced in each subsequent unit. I thoroughly recommend reading Unit 1 first, exploring and embedding its content, and getting that all settled in, before moving on to the next unit. Give it a week to ten days. Don't be in a hurry. If hurry is your habit, now is a good time to slow down and smell the roses.

......

'THE ABILITY TO BE IN THE PRESENT MOMENT IS A MAJOR COMPONENT OF MENTAL WELLNESS.'

......

Abraham Maslow

In each of Units 2–7, we will introduce one of the six **Competencies of EQ**, the underlying science of that component, and how it applies to your daily life.

We will also learn six **Mindful Moment** techniques, making it easier for you to integrate simple but profound habits that will rewire your nervous system and shift your inner landscape in the direction of greater presence, health and success. There are six **Power Tools**, techniques to get you out of a jam and free you up.

Finally, In Unit 8 we will bring all the pieces together, take stock and explore what's next.

What you end up with is a **Resource Kit** for winning at the game of life – you won't be happier, or better, but you'll be more at peace with yourself, more whole.

As I said, some parts will resonate with you more strongly than others. Fine. Just make sure that you are consistent in your Daily Formal Practice. When you fall off the wagon or let things slide, no matter. Just climb back on again.

Most of all, I really hope you have some fun! Make the book your own. Draw, colour, write, scribble. When you look back I hope that you will see a document that represents an exciting, creative and life-enhancing journey. We take ourselves so seriously these days, and maybe that's part of the problem. Having travelled widely, I've seen that some of the most wholesome people have very little, except perhaps a deep sense of self and a broad smile.

••••••
'LIFE IS A DARING ADVENTURE OR NOTHING AT ALL.'
••••••

George Bernard Shaw

UNIT 1

• • • • • •

- **The Science Bit:** Brainwaves and the prefrontal cortex
- **Mindful Moment:** Press 'Pause'
- **Mindfulness:** The Daily Formal Practice – how and why
- **Motto:** 'I am not my thoughts; I *have* thoughts.'
- **Skill Set for Health:** Generosity
- **Homework:** In the flow

••••••

The science bit

If I were to put electrodes on your head, they would pick up the electromagnetic activity in your brain. This activity represents the conversations going on between millions of nerve cells in your brain's neurons. Once picked up by the electrodes, the activity can be visualized on a monitor, as waveforms that look something like this:

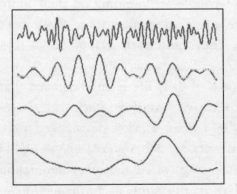

Beta waves: 12hz–38hz
Wide awake

Alpha waves: 8hz–12hz
Awake but relaxed

Theta waves: 3hz–8hz
Light sleep or extreme relaxation

Delta waves: 0.2hz–3hz
Deep, dreamless sleep

In the normal waking state, we exhibit predominantly beta wave activity. Our minds are whirring away analysing the constant stream of data and information coming our way, judging and categorizing the input on the basis of past experience so we can negotiate our way through it all and make sense of the world.

When we are under pressure – say, when a report or essay needs finishing to a deadline – we can ramp up brain functioning, thanks in part to a chemical called adrenaline. With this high-level beta wave activity, we become super-productive for a couple of hours. It's like pulling out the fuel injection button on your car to turbo-charge the engine when you want to overtake that idiot stuck in the middle lane on the motorway.

Here's the thing. You would never leave your car in turbo-charge mode because the engine would burn out. But these days, millions of people are ramping up their brain engines into overdrive and getting stuck there. They can't find the 'Off' button. They can't even change down to a lower gear.

The pressure and speed of daily life seem to demand that we are constantly in overdrive. Overdrive starts to feel normal and we feel really odd when we slow down, even a bit. People wear their long working hours and sleepless nights like a badge of honour, using coffee and other adrenaline fixes to keep themselves in this super-performance mode. The work culture rewards such behaviour and makes invisible the suffering it brings.

The result? Stress, exhaustion, burnout. Anxiety, depression, addictive behaviours.

......

'WE TREAT OUR CARS AND SMARTPHONES BETTER THAN WE TREAT OURSELVES, TAKING THEM IN FOR HEALTH CHECKS, MAKING SURE THAT THEY HAVE THE RIGHT FUEL, PLUGGING THEM IN TO RECHARGE.'

......

To take better care of ourselves and function more effectively, we need to dial down through the gears regularly, slow down the brainwaves to low beta and alpha. During alpha wave activity, analytical, judgemental, logical thinking gives way to a gentler, more creative and more effective way of operating. Brain and body systems start to synchronize, become more coherent and more energy-efficient. Life feels less effortful. We find our flow. Top athletes function in flow – in alpha wave mode – responding accurately and effectively in the moment without thinking.

The Mindful Moments and Daily Formal Practice outlined in this book help you dial down the stress, move through the gears to a more balanced, clearer state that benefits cognitive functioning, creativity and emotional balance.

Small children live predominantly in an even slower mode – characterized by theta waves. They absorb the world without critical analysis or rationality. This means kids absorb what they are told without question. They soak up everything that comes their way, without judgement. In particular, they soak up the emotional ambience of their main environment, which becomes their normal.

The slowest level of brain activity is delta wave, when we are deeply asleep. If you're overtired, you might find that there is a tendency to plummet quickly into delta waves when you first start the Daily Formal Practice. If this is the case, you need to get more sleep! By the way, you will find you sleep better once you get in to a regular Daily Formal Practice routine.

Here's a diagram that summarizes all this:

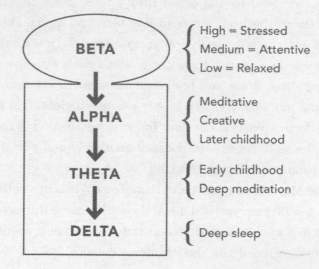

BETA
{ High = Stressed
Medium = Attentive
Low = Relaxed

ALPHA
{ Meditative
Creative
Later childhood

THETA
{ Early childhood
Deep meditation

DELTA
{ Deep sleep

Mindful Moment: Press 'pause'

Let's take some time out right now to dial down the brain-waves and practise the first Mindful Moment – Press 'Pause'. Do it first as you read the instructions, then do it again on your own.

PRESS 'PAUSE'

Feel your feet on the ground. Notice exactly where your feet are in contact with the ground and what that feels like. Release your shoulders and release your jaw. Soften your eyes. Pull up through your spine from the base of your pelvis all the way up to your neck. Just for this moment, stop. Nothing to do, nowhere to go. Breathe in a little more deeply and slowly than usual. Exhale slowly. Do this three times more, four breaths in all. Notice how you feel.

• • • • • •

PRESS 'PAUSE' THROUGHOUT YOUR DAY TODAY. MAKE IT A HABIT.

• • • • • •

Thoughts

We have between 50,000 and 90,000 thoughts a day. Most of them are the same, or variations on a theme, and most of them go unnoticed – a background hum that colours our experience of ourselves and the world around us. Stop now and listen.

What thoughts are going through your head right now? Mine are like chattering monkeys. What are the chattering monkeys in your head saying right now? 'What monkeys? I don't have any chatter in my head!' you may be thinking. That's your chatter! It's going on all the time, mostly unconsciously. By stopping and directing our attention to something as simple and real as our breath, we start to notice this background chatter more and distinguish it for what it is – thoughts, coming and going like the weather.

We don't experience reality; we interpret it. We interpret it through a filter of beliefs, attitudes, patterns of thought, assumptions and understandings that are represented in the brain by well-trodden neural pathways. If we can start to hear this background hum, we start to notice more about what our personal interpretation of reality is.

This filter system is like software uploaded during the course of our lives, mainly in childhood. When your teacher told you that you were not creative, you didn't have the critical faculties to retort 'Hang on a minute – how are you defining creativity?' You simply absorbed this 'factoid' into your software as a facet of who you are – *not creative*.

In one of the courses I was running, we were discussing this and a participant told us about his wife, who's a professional singer. She'd come home from a particularly successful gig and was on the telephone to her mum telling her about her evening. 'But, darling,' her mum told her, 'you're no good at singing.' Interesting!

When I was four, I invited family members to a concert I was going to put on at the bottom of the garden. Standing on a log, I was in full swing with Harry Belafonte's 'The Banana Boat Song' when my granddad called out, 'Oh, Barbie, you do look stupid.' Thanks, Granddad. OK, so in my flow, being totally myself, I looked stupid. Better not do that again then.

These are the things our subconscious is made of. The experiences that get wired into our brains and shape our sense of self, the filters through which we perceive ourselves and the world.

You go on a date. It doesn't work out. 'I'm unlovable,' says the belief-programmed chatter in your head. The central heating breaks down. 'Why does this always happen to me? I'm such a loser,' says the voice in your head, on repeat, like a stuck needle on a vinyl record.

Playing Monopoly last Christmas one of my daughters got a 'Go to jail' card. Twice in a row. 'I'm so unlucky,' she said as she threw a double six. Twice in a row! We see what we want to see, so 'reality' fits into our beliefs about ourselves and the world. We focus on the 'Go to jail' card and ignore the double sixes. And the chattering monkeys are there to remind us of such negativity. Until we realize that they are just chattering monkeys, thoughts on repeat, they can have a profound impact on our lives.

An interesting place to start being more aware of this background hum, the chattering monkeys of your mind, is to eavesdrop on the conversation they are having in your head when you look at yourself in the mirror.

Write in this box things you've been told about yourself by others, and things you tell yourself about yourself. Keep adding to it as we go through the book. As you improve your ability to notice your chattering monkeys, you will notice more and more of this subconscious script and, in so doing, be freed from it.

To be clear, we're not trying to drive out the chattering monkeys, just alter our relationship with them. The more you let them be, the more they will let you be.

Motto:

......

'I AM NOT MY
THOUGHTS; I HAVE
THOUGHTS.'

......

Subconscious script

A participant on an MMM course, a banker in the City of London – let's call him Fred – noticed that every time his boss walked into the open-plan office, his palms got sweaty, his pulse started racing and the chattering monkeys started up with a familiar patter. 'She didn't like that report. I knew I should have worked harder on it. She's coming over. Oh God, that pile of papers is for me! Maybe I'm going to get fired.' As the boss walked on by, Fred calmed down and realized that this mental-emotional pattern of sweaty palms, panic and self-criticism had been entirely his own creation.

On closer inspection, he realized that the boss reminded him of a particularly vindictive teacher at his boarding school who had made his life hell. Stashed away in his subconscious script were memories and beliefs uploaded into his software during that time, through which he was now, unwittingly, interpreting this situation. It was an example of unconscious bias.

Simply by realizing this, he started to free himself from the pattern. Noticing the reactions he was having – the bodily sensations, feelings and thoughts – he also noticed the underlying belief system: 'I'm such a failure.' The external reality showed us a successful city banker. But his internal reality and experience of himself bore no relationship to the external reality. With that belief system, 'I'm such a failure', running the show, nothing he did would ever be good enough for him to experience himself as successful.

By altering his relationship to the repetitive chatter in his head, he was no longer run by it. 'I am not my thoughts; I *have* thoughts.' By personifying these thoughts as the conversation of chattering monkeys, his own creation, they no longer ran him. He had made friends with his chattering monkeys.

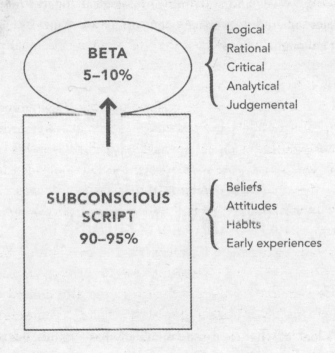

Presence dissolves the unconscious past. By increasing his self-awareness, the ability to notice and allow, in the present, the sensations, feelings and thoughts as they rise and fall, he unpicked and released himself from the prison of a chunk of his history.

We all have this subconscious script going on. It's inevitable. By doing the Daily Formal Practice, and taking Mindful Moments, we are giving ourselves the opportunity to notice the script, see it for what it is, and choose. We slow down the brainwaves and shift our physiological state to one of greater coherence. A space opens up as we realize, 'This is just a thought.'

......

`A SPACE OPENS UP AS WE REALIZE, "THIS IS JUST A THOUGHT."'

......

Let's look at what we can do on a daily basis to exercise our brains in a way that works – the Daily Formal Practice.

Daily Formal Practice

We'll break this down into four phases.

1. PREPARATION: The three Ps – Place, Posture and Poise

Place: Take the time to prepare a place where you go every day to practise, a place where you can sit quietly and comfortably in a firm chair. Habit thrives on repetition. Your new habit will develop better if you repeat the same procedures in the same way in the same place, and ideally at the same time in your daily routine. If you're not at home right now, imagine where in your home would be a good spot. When will you go there? Imagine it happening now.

Posture: Once seated, take a minute to organize your body. Place your feet hip-width apart, fair and square on the ground. Place your knees parallel to one another and hip-width apart, and your hands resting palms down on your thighs. Push your bottom backwards in the chair so that you are fully supported and pull up through your spine. Do a few shoulder rolls in both directions. Move your head to free up your neck. Soften through the front of the body so that you can breathe more freely. Take your time. Land in an awareness of your body.

(Wherever you are right now, do this simple posture adjustment. Changing your posture has a profound effect on your mental and emotional functioning.)

Poise: Approach your practice, this daily gift to yourself, with a sense of dignity and poise. Take a moment to gather yourself as you sit on the chair.

2. DOING IT

Now you've got the place all set, your body nicely lined up, and your attitude sorted, set your timer for ten minutes. Close your eyes and open them very slightly so that you can see the floor immediately ahead of you. Soften your gaze, soften your eyes, release your shoulders. Let go of your jaw. Let your tongue lie heavy in your mouth. Notice your breathing. Focus your attention on your breathing. Follow the cycle of your breath. In breath, out breath. Be curious about that cycle.

Focus strongly on holding your attention on your breath. Every time you notice that you have wandered away and are lost in thought, firmly but gently bring your attention back to following the cycle of your breath.

In doing this, you are exercising powerful mental muscles that alter the way your brain is wired for the better. When the timer signals the end of your session, take a moment to stretch, compose yourself, look around the room. Don't be in a rush.

3. STAY PRESENT

When you get up from the chair, notice how you feel. Anchor that sense of yourself in your memory. Aim to maintain that sense of space and calm.

Notice anything that might throw you out of that state. The phone rings, an email pings in, someone asks you a difficult question... 'Dammit!' you say to yourself. 'Now look what you've done. Broken my peacefulness!'

In that moment you have a choice: regain your composure or go down route autopilot.

4. KEEP IT UP

Practice this every day. Even if it's on the train, bus or in your chair at work, make time every day to spend a few minutes focusing on your breath.

Why?

Why do this? What is the purpose? What is the intention?

The intention behind this Daily Formal Practice may be to reduce stress, to free up space around a particular problem, or to get beyond the sense of needing external validation to feel OK about yourself. Sometimes it can simply be because it feels so good afterwards. Sometimes it can be about accessing a place of tranquillity and authenticity within oneself.

When your chattering monkeys say 'Not today, no need, no time, can't be bothered, it doesn't work anyway,' or words to that effect, thank them for sharing their opinion with you and do it anyway, because you said you would.

Make a daily appointment with yourself and put it in your calendar. Keep your commitment to yourself no matter what. Notice the chatter in your head that might try and dissuade you from keeping your promise to yourself. 'It's too late now.' 'I'm too tired.' 'I'll do it tomorrow.' 'I can't be bothered.' And so on...

If you can do it for 11 days straight, you are building a powerful new and beneficial habit into the wiring in your brain. Use the Daily Game Record Sheet to help you.

To help you record your progress, download the *Mindfulness Playbook* Weekly Record Sheet from here: www.teachyourself.com/downloads.

A bit more science

The newest part of our brains from an evolutionary perspective is the prefrontal cortex (PFC). This is the seat of our self-awareness and is a bit like our chief executive officer. Being at speed means being adrenaline-driven, in high-level beta wave mode. To engage CEO functioning, we need to slow down...

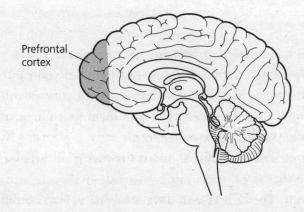

Prefrontal cortex

The brain changes shape according to how you use it. This is great news. We can intentionally change our brain and nervous system for the better. Regularly using the Mindful Moments and the Daily Formal Practice, the CEO prefrontal cortex increases in size and activity, particularly on the left side (LPFC), promoting greater self-awareness, the essential building block for emotional intelligence. We are giving ourselves a mental and emotional upgrade.

Please note these diagrams of the brain are illustrative rather than anatomically exact.

......

'WE CAN INTENTIONALLY CHANGE OUR BRAIN AND NERVOUS SYSTEM FOR THE BETTER.'

......

Choice

As you go about your daily life, start to notice the thoughts that are going on in your head. The moment you can notice that you are having thoughts rather than being absorbed in them as if they were real, you are opening up a space that allows greater choice and freedom.

So much of our internal distress comes from believing the chatter that goes on in our heads rather than bearing witness to it. The chatter will always be there. It's our relationship to it that alters.

Sitting every day with the intention to pull your attention away from your thoughts and back to something that is real and happening now – for example, your breath – upgrades those CEO brain muscles and makes noticing these chattering monkeys easier. We get better at coming off autopilot, being present and exercising choice.

Remember our Unit 1 motto:

·······

'I AM NOT MY THOUGHTS; I HAVE THOUGHTS'

·······

Skill Set for Health: Generosity

In each unit we will explore a different Skill Set for Health theme, all of which upgrade whole person wellbeing. The theme for this unit is generosity.

People who are generous have greater life satisfaction and live longer. When we are generous, chemical changes take place that have us feel better about ourselves and about others, so we are literally generating our own wellness. Doing good does you good.

True generosity comes from a sense of abundance, openness and a genuine unconditional desire to contribute, without any sense of resentment, burden, obligation or need for recognition. What do you feel like when you are generous? Generosity includes smiling at a stranger, giving a helping hand on the bus or tube, performing a spontaneous act of kindness or saying a well-wishing word that can have an impact way beyond what you can imagine.

For the next week, stick up yellow stickies around the place with the word 'generosity' on them. If anyone asks why you're doing this, tell them that you're boosting your wellness battery. Remind yourself every morning. Use the *Mindfulness Playbook* Record Sheet. At the end of the day, make a note of how you were generous and what happened as a result.

Download the *Mindfulness Playbook* Weekly Record Sheet from here: www.teachyourself.com/downloads.

Homework: In the flow

The homework for this unit is to write about a time when you were fully engaged in something and had the sense of really being yourself, in your flow. You were so absorbed in what you were doing that time flew by. You may have had the feeling 'This is the real me.' You felt energized, relaxed, fulfilled and at ease. What were you doing? What were you wearing? Where were you? Who was there? Recreate the experience.

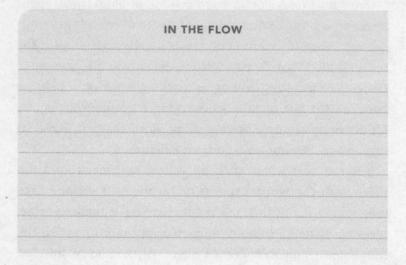

IN THE FLOW

When you've described this event, take a good look at what you have written. What strengths and natural aptitudes were you displaying at that time?

When we're 'in the flow', we are usually using talents and abilities that seem so easy and obvious to us that we may not even realize that they are strengths or aptitudes. It's a bit like that game where someone sticks a yellow stickie on your forehead and you have to guess who it is. Everyone else can see it but you can't. When it comes to yourself, what qualities or gifts would be written on that yellow stickie? Ask those who know you well what they think.

......

'OUR GREATEST POTENTIAL FOR SUCCESS IS TO BUILD ON WHO YOU ALREADY ARE. YOU CANNOT BE ANYTHING YOU WANT TO BE BUT YOU CAN BE A LOT MORE OF WHO YOU ALREADY ARE.'

......

Tom Rath

Strengths, innate talents and abilities are different from things we've learned to be good at. The key difference is the sense of exhilaration, effortlessness and energy that comes with exercising your natural aptitudes. Ideally, you want to make these inherent qualities the pillars around which you build your life – that is, you should build your life around what you already naturally *are*, your implicit design.

Sometimes we lose touch with this or forget. 'Life', with

all its obligations and all the things we 'have to' do, takes over. So it's good to remind ourselves of who we really are.

Actually, it's essential for whole person wellbeing. Play to your strengths.

UNIT 2

• • • • • •

- **The science bit:** The amygdala and the autonomic nervous system (ANS)
- **Mindfulness:** Noticing and focusing
- **Mindful Moment:** USB – Unplug. Slow down. Breathe.
- **Motto:** 'Nothing means anything except the meaning I give it.'
- **EQ Competence:** Bounce-back
- **Power Tool:** BELL – Breathe. Expand. Listen. Look.
- **Skill Set for Health:** Appreciation
- **Homework:** Thank-you letter

••••••

Arrgghh!

In Unit 1 we talked about how we don't experience reality; rather, we interpret it through our very own unique filter of beliefs, attitudes and habits. Some of these are shared among social, cultural, political, class and family groupings. Others are derived from our own life experience.

In this unit we're going to explore what your triggers are, what stresses you out and, more importantly, what you can do about it. ... Oh, and how that all works in the body and brain.

One belief that seems to underpin most people's filter systems in the Western world is 'I'm not OK. There's something wrong with me.' It's a bit surprising to realize that people from other cultures do not have such self-destructive thought processes dominating their internal chatter.

This information can be as shocking to some people as the realization that the world was not flat was to people four centuries ago. In other words, could the deep-seated question 'What's wrong with me?' that lies beneath so much existential angst be nothing more than a sociocultural construct? Now there is an interesting thought.

••••••

'THE MOST EXCITING BREAKTHROUGHS OF
THE TWENTY-FIRST CENTURY WILL NOT
OCCUR BECAUSE OF TECHNOLOGY, BUT
BECAUSE OF AN EXPANDED CONCEPT OF
WHAT IT MEANS TO BE HUMAN.'

••••••

John Naisbitt

Let's dial up the focus for a moment on what is it that gets your goat, winds you up, or slowly, drip by drip, erodes your energy. What causes you to get anxious, tight, irritated, wound up, edgy, miserable, dejected, tired, bored? Which people? What situations? Take some time now to think about this and write them down in the box on the next page. The clearer you are about your triggers, the more you can gain mastery of them.

In this box write down all the things that trigger you. What gets you stressed? What plugs you in, makes you angry, upset, anxious, feel small, not your true self? Write them down in this box. Dump them right here. You can add to this box any time you want.

Now we're going to turn our attention to what happens inside you. What does being stressed, anxious, angry, upset, etc. feel like? What thoughts do you have?

What sensations do you experience in your body? Sweaty palms? Fluttery tummy? Heart pounding? Tightness in the chest, jaw, shoulders, neck, tummy, legs, feet?

What feelings and thoughts arise? Do you shrink into a smaller sense of yourself or explode outwards? Do you feel sad, anxious, angry? Does your brain seem to freeze up? What thoughts go through your head? 'Silly idiot!', 'Jeez, people are so ...', 'Why am I so useless?', 'I wish I could just run away', etc.

We're going to leave all that there for a minute or two and look at a model to explain what we are doing in our Daily Formal Practice and Mindful Moments. And then we will

51

explore some of the science behind what happens when we get triggered. Finally, we'll discover a powerful tool to regain presence and balance.

Noticing and focusing

Imagine a bicycle. The two wheels of the bicycle are **Noticing** and **Focusing**: noticing what is going on in our sensations, feelings and thoughts, and focusing our attention intentionally where we choose to put it.

In our Daily Formal Practice, we focus on our breath as a real-time activity in our body. We bring our mind and body together, as we follow the cycle of breathing.

Then we notice that we've drifted off and our attention is now on our thoughts. We allow the thoughts to be, without judgement – neither good thoughts nor bad thoughts, but just *thoughts*. Focus back on the breath. And so they go round, the two wheels of the mindfulness bicycle.

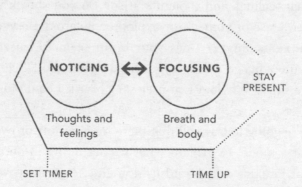

We may not even realize we've drifted off for quite a while. 'Lost in thought' is a very familiar place to be, a very powerful unconscious habit. We seem to love replaying and ruminating on things that have happened, and fast-forwarding, worrying about what might happen in the future. The moment we catch ourselves, when we notice the chattering monkeys at work, we intentionally drag our attention away from that train of thought, no matter how juicy and enticing it might be, and focus back on something real, something happening now, our breath.

Notice your background hum, the chattering monkey thoughts, right now. Cultivate an accepting and kind attitude to them, and thereby to yourself. We are training our minds to be more focused, and to be able to notice sooner when we are no longer present. Without judgement.

As we increase this skill of self-awareness, the left prefrontal cortex (LPFC) gets stronger. In Unit 6 we will see more about why this is so important. In addition, over time, a part of the brain called the amygdala gets less reactive. We become less prone to reacting with anxiety, anger or tension to the circumstances of life. Our inner landscape becomes more peaceful.

•••••••

'I'VE EXPERIENCED SOME TERRIBLE THINGS IN MY LIFE, A COUPLE OF WHICH ACTUALLY HAPPENED.'

•••••••

Mark Twain

The science bit

THE AMYGDALA

The amygdala is a tiny but crucial part of our brain that is like our very own Neighbourhood Watch. There are actually two, one on each side of the brain, but we tend to refer to it in the singular. The amygdala is constantly subliminally vigilant, picking up anything that threatens our survival in any way. One hundred thousand years ago this might have been a hairy mammoth or a tiger, a very real and tangible threat.

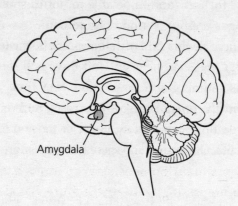

Amygdala

Before we register a threat consciously, the amygdala picks up the implicit danger, and starts a cascade reaction of chemicals in the body, the fight or flight response. Adrenaline and cortisol flood the system to raise blood pressure, heart rate, breathing and blood sugar, and divert blood away from the gut to our muscles, so we are ready to fight with all our might or run like the wind. Cortisol inhibits the immune system, healing and fertility. There's no time for those things when our survival is at stake.

All resources are channelled on facing the threat and overcoming it. Muscles get tight: jaw, shoulders, breathing, stomach. Cognitive functioning locks in on what is menacing us. Everything contracts, even our sense of ourselves.

We are in survival mode. Co-operation, listening and empathy go out the window. The number-one priority is to protect number one. This is the basis of the stress response.

AUTONOMIC NERVOUS SYSTEM

Most of the automatic functions of our body are governed by the autonomic nervous system (ANS). A rich network of interdependent systems is constantly adjusting our internal milieu to maintain homeostasis, or inner balance, in the body – encompassing body temperature, blood sugar levels, flow of blood to vital organs such as the brain and kidneys, and heart rate.

The ANS has two operating modes. One is the **sympathetic** mode. This gets activated by the amygdala when we're under threat; it's the so-called 'fight or flight' response. The other is the **parasympathetic** mode, which activates the 'rest and digest' response. The vagus nerve, which travels through most of the internal organs of the body, is an important mediator of this response. When vagus nerve activity dominates, the brain interprets this as 'All is well. There is no threat out there, and we can go into cruise control and relax.'

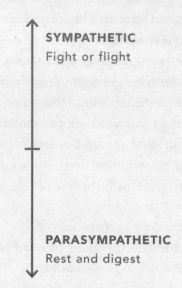

SYMPATHETIC
Fight or flight

PARASYMPATHETIC
Rest and digest

THE BAD NEWS

In an ideal world, the two modes synchronize well and there is an appropriate balance between them. However, when we are chronically stressed, or running on empty, the sympathetic mode dominates. We are run by adrenaline and have higher levels of cortisol in our bodies than we need. The overproduction of these two essential body chemicals is the cause of untold modern-day physical ailments.

These days the biggest source of threat is the sheer speed of daily life and the incessant tsunami of information with which we are deluged. The second biggest trigger for the stress response is our own interpretation of reality, our own thinking.

As we saw in Unit 1, we don't experience reality, we interpret it through our filter system. There is seldom a real threat out there but our interpretation tells us that there is. That interpretation gets us caught up in repetitive and habit-driven loops of thoughts and feelings, what Eckhart Tolle calls **mental–emotional reaction patterns**. (There's more on this in Unit 3.)

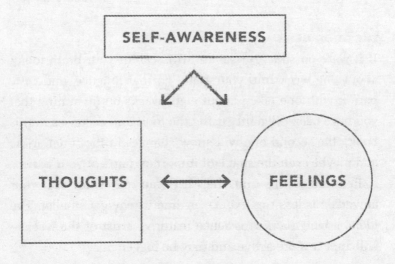

There are often very real and challenging circumstances in our lives. But our interpretation and habitual ways of reacting to them can hinder our ability to deal with them appropriately and effectively. We may well be under a lot of pressure in the external circumstances of our lives, at home or at work. However, it's how we engage with these challenges that determines their ultimate impact. In this book, we are learning more effective ways to operate.

......

'INSANITY IS DOING THE SAME THING OVER AND OVER AGAIN AND EXPECTING A DIFFERENT RESULT.'

......

Albert Einstein

THE GOOD NEWS

If it were possible to take an MRI scan of your brain today, about one week into your Daily Formal Practice, and compare it with one taken about eight weeks on (assuming that you have been diligently using the tools and exercises in this book), the second one will show changes in the functioning and maybe even the shape of important parts of your brain.

Relevant to this unit, the MRI scan may show that your amygdala is less reactive. Over time it may get smaller. The LPFC – Unit 1's neuroscience featured 'artist of the week' – will appear more active and may be bigger.

In addition, the richness of neural connections between the two will be greater. The LPFC, our CEO, is communicating more with the Neighbourhood Watch amygdala. This has profound implications for our day-to-day functioning, making us less reactive, and enabling us to regain composure better when we do. We are more able to discern real from imagined threats, and see how our own interpretation may be the source of, or adding to, our upset.

EQ Competence: Bounce-back

Bounce-back is our first EQ Competence, as based on the pioneering work of Richard Davidson and described in his wonderful book *The Emotional Life of Your Brain*. According to the professor's research, there is a correlation between our ability to recover from setbacks, challenges and real or imagined threats, and the thickness of the neural pathways between CEO and Neighbourhood Watch – LPFC and amygdala.

How quickly do you bounce back from a tricky conversation? Do you tend to replay it in your mind, hold on to the grievance, or even escalate it in your imagination as you replay it? Do you regurgitate conversations or events and torture yourself with clever things you could have said? If there's a setback at work, someone else gets the promotion you wanted, or you make a mistake that has consequences for others, how quickly do you get back to a sense of equilibrium within yourself?

People with high Bounce-back take a longer time to get over 'stuff' than people with low Bounce-back. They bounce high in terms of their reaction to things and it takes them a while to 'land', recover, to let go, learn and move on. What Richardson's research showed is that they will probably have weaker and/or fewer neural pathways between CEO/LPFC and NW/amygdala. People who have low Bounce-back and land back on the ground, composed and balanced, quicker after an upset have richer connections between LPFC and amygdala.

The really good news is that the brain changes shape according to how you use it – this is called the brain's **neuroplasticity**.

By following the Daily Formal Practice, Mindful Moments and the Skill Set for Health themes in this book you are increasing the density and functionality of the neural pathways between LPFC and amygdala, between CEO and Neighbourhood Watch, moving your current set point towards lower, better Bounce-back.

The result is better emotional intelligence, or EQ. EQ and stress are inversely proportional. Less stress equals more EQ.

......

'LESS STRESS EQUALS MORE EQ.'

......

When the amygdala is on red alert, we are in survival mode. Our senses are channelled towards the threat, real or imagined, and to that alone. We have tunnel vision and locked-in hearing. Our body processes are speeded up, and we are hyper-vigilant for danger and ready to flip.

To be able to respond intelligently, we need to be present – balanced and in touch with ourselves, our inner core, and what we are experiencing in this moment. We are able to read, interpret and translate input and respond appropriately and effectively. The better our Bounce-Back, the quicker we bring ourselves back to our Inner Core, and the greater our emotional intelligence.

In summary, our ability to let go, move on and assimilate past experiences in a constructive way is proportional to the strength of the wiring between CEO and NW. And we can strengthen that wiring intentionally. We can improve our emotional intelligence and equip ourselves to better deal with the challenges life throws us.

Notice what you are making things mean, and ask yourself 'Is that so?'

Motto:

• • • • • •

'NOTHING MEANS
ANYTHING EXCEPT
THE MEANING
I GIVE IT.'

• • • • • •

Mindful Moments: USB

So far we've practised Press 'Pause'. Now we're going to introduce another Mindful Moment, USB. – Unplug. Slow down. Breathe.

Whenever you think of it, and particularly if you notice you are getting tense, anxious, irritated, or off balance, make a note to yourself to take a deep breath in and feel your feet on the ground.

......

UNPLUG.
SLOW DOWN.
BREATHE.

......

Anchor this Mindful Moment to a trigger in your daily life. This could be your phone: every time you reach for your phone, use this as a reminder to be present – to Unplug, Slow down, Breathe.

Using the Mindful Moments, we are building up more self-awareness and exercising the 'muscle' of presence throughout the day. Like any skill, the more we do it, the easier it gets.

Power Tool: Bell

Our first Power Tool is BELL – Breathe. Expand. Listen. Look.

Whenever you feel you are not present, ring your BELL. Close your eyes for a moment and get an image of a bell. Draw it in this box.

BELL

Use this Power Tool whenever you think of it. And particularly when you feel you are getting stressed, frazzled or upset, anything that leads into 'brain freeze'. Ring your BELL:

- **Breathe:** Take a deep breath in and exhale slowly. This slows down the brain waves, stimulates the vagus nerve and parasympathetic side of your ANS, and alters your physiological state.

- **Expand:** Say the word 'expand' to yourself. This allows you to notice more of what is happening, releases tension in the body and expands your sense of yourself.

- **Listen:** What can you hear right now? What else? Widen your horizon. Widen your perceptual field. Come to your senses.

- **Look:** Really look at something, describe it to yourself, focus on what is present, something real.

When we are upset, we develop tunnel vision and locked-in hearing. We lock into the source of upset. We get smaller in our sense of ourselves. **Small Self** is in survival mode, looking out for number one.

By saying the word 'expand', we intentionally widen our perceptual field to include more of what is going on. We expand our perspective, which gives rise to new possibilities, better ways of responding. We expand our awareness and feeling about ourselves. **Expanded Self** is open, generous and creative, functions better cognitively and makes wiser decisions.

Choice goes out the window when we get upset because

we go into survival mode. BELL allows us to reconnect with the bigger picture, engage CEO functioning and connect to core values. Your nervous system gets used to being in better balance and that becomes the norm.

When you notice you're lost in thought, ruminating about something that's already happened, getting upset about a current situation, or worrying about something that might never happen, ring your BELL. Bring yourself back to Now. Let the thoughts and feelings be. They will pass, like the weather. Everything does.

Ring your BELL when you're walking to work, on the train, in a meeting. Cut through the chatter in your head. Practice bringing yourself back to the here and now.

Be especially aware of ringing your BELL. when you get triggered. Cut through the stress response, alter your physiological state, stimulate your vagus nerve and the parasympathetic side of your ANS.

USING THE BELL

Go back to one of the triggers you wrote in the box earlier – a situation that plugs you in, makes you upset. Conjure it up in your imagination. Close your eyes if that helps. Remind yourself of what happens and how that feels. What happens in your body? Now ring your BELL. Unwind your body, pull yourself up through the spine.

From this calmer, more collected sense of self, see what options you have. See what possibilities might arise and how you being present and calm changes the situation that habitually triggers you.

Practise doing this with sticky situations in your imagination ahead of time. You will behave differently when that situation actually arises. You are training your brain to be more effective in the face of fire.

Sometimes we have to ring the BELL several times to calm ourselves down and get to the other side of an upset. Have the intention to bring mindful self-awareness to even challenging situations.

Skill Set for Health: Appreciation

The Skill Set for Health theme for this unit is appreciation. Appreciation is one of the most powerfully restorative emotional states there is.

We tend to focus on what we don't have and what's missing from our lives, the stuff that goes wrong. We can thank our amygdala for that, as it's always on the lookout for danger. We miss the good stuff that is right under our noses.

••••••

'THE GOLDEN MOMENTS IN THE STREAM OF
LIFE RUSH PAST US AND WE SEE BUT SAND.
THE ANGELS COME TO VISIT US, AND WE
ONLY KNOW THEM WHEN THEY ARE GONE.'

••••••

George Eliot

Developing our ability to be appreciative shifts the way we see the world and alters our brain's shape and wiring. Chemical changes occur in the body when we experience and express appreciation, changes that reduce stress and promote wellbeing. And it's contagious, so everyone wins.

Whatever we focus on gets bigger, gets more energy. When we focus on what goes wrong – what's wrong with us, what's wrong with our lives – that gets bigger. It takes conscious choice and courage to drag ourselves away from this tendency to see the worst. That's what this Skill Set for Health theme is about: training ourselves to also see what is working; actively seeking out and noticing the good in our lives, and choosing to focus our attention, intentionally, on that.

As we do this, we create an upward spiral. The more we look for what is good, the more we see that. Our view of reality and of ourselves subtly shifts. As Wayne Dyer said, 'When we change the way we look at things, the things we look at change.'

To help you record your progress, download the *Mindfulness Playbook* Weekly Record Sheet from here: www.teachyourself.com/downloads.

· Homework: Thank-you letter

The homework for Unit 2 is to think of someone who has made a contribution to your life. Write them a thank-you letter. Say specifically what you want to thank them for, what difference they made to your life, and how it supported you. If possible, give them this letter in person so you can talk about it once they've read it. These seemingly small gestures can make a profound difference, for you and for the recipient.

UNIT 3

• • • • • •

- **The Science Bit:** The insula
- **Mindfulness:** Presence through movement
- **Mindful Moment:** SMS – Stretch. Move. Sigh.
- **Motto:** 'We don't experience reality, we interpret it.'
- **EQ Competence:** Somatic awareness
- **Power Tool:** BREATH
- **Skill Set for Health:** Acceptance
- **Homework:** 'WWW?' Journal

• • • • • •

Choice-fulness

Mindfulness is a funny word. Full of mind – what does that mean? Aren't we trying to empty the mind? Well, no. You can't. If you were to be totally present and fully in your experience, how would you 'know' that, other than by separating yourself from it and having the thought 'Oh, I'm not having any thoughts'? Uh-oh, as my grandson would say. Catch-22. It's not about emptying the mind. It's about transforming our relationship to its content.

In Unit 2, we explored how automatic our reactions can be, based on the past. Our beliefs, attitudes, habits and patterns of behaviour, which are wired into the circuitry of our brains, can make it hard to do otherwise. And we saw how stress makes it more likely that we will operate in autopilot mode. Stress shuts down our higher brain centres, narrows our cognitive functioning, floods our system with chemicals that put us on red alert, and contracts our experiential sense of self. We become our Small Self.

In Unit 2 we also learned about the BELL Power Tool – Breathe. Expand. Listen. Look. This simple tool brings us back to the here and now. In essence, 'ringing' the BELL slows things down and buys us time. Rather than us resorting to habit-driven, knee-jerk patterns of behaviour, presence opens up the possibility of choice.

Mind the gap

Every action is a reaction to a previous input or stimulus. Input, be it from the environment, or our own inner world, prompts an output, or reaction, in the shape of a sensation, feeling, thought or action.

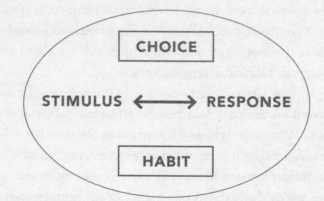

This, of course, is an oversimplified cognitive model of human behaviour. There is much more to being human than this. But for now it helps us get to grips with a very useful concept. The more frazzled we are, the more automaticity takes over. We see the disastrous consequences of this automaticity in the shooting of more than a thousand people in the United States in 2015, some of them unarmed, many of them African American males, and many of them killed without due cause. A policeman in survival mode is on red alert. The amygdala is running the show. Unconscious bias rules and that's not OK.

In Scotland, where policemen do not carry firearms, they've developed a strategy to deal with people who are a threat – for example a man wielding a machete – without bloodshed. They have a plan. In other words, they engage CEO functioning, work together as a team and maximize presence. This counteracts unconscious bias and brings balance and common sense back into the picture.

Let's go back to our stimulus–response model and take a look at more everyday scenarios.

A stimulus can arise externally or internally:

- **External stimulus:** Someone in the kitchen at work says, 'Why isn't there any coffee left in the jar?' Your physical response includes a raised heart rate and tension in jaw and stomach. You feel irritated. You have the thought, 'That's because *you* didn't pay your money into the kitty.' Your action is to retort somewhat sarcastically, 'I wonder!' and then leave.

- **Internal stimulus:** You have the thought 'I'm such an idiot. Why can't I do this?' In response, sensations in your body include a sinking feeling in your stomach, a slumping of your posture and heaviness in your chest. You feel sad and/or anxious. The further thought 'I have to get away – maybe I should quit' arises. Because you are immobilized and drained of energy, it's hard to act.

The interplay of stimulus and response can lead to a **chain reaction**. For example, the external stimulus might be that the printer won't work. Your response is the thought 'Why can't I fix this? I'm such an idiot', which goes on to act as an internal stimulus – a sinking feeling in your stomach, a slumping of your posture and heaviness in your chest. You feel sad and/or anxious. So you think, 'I hate my job...' And so on.

Eckhart Tolle called these endless loops we get tied up in **Mental–Emotional Reaction Patterns** (MERPs for short). An input stimulates a sensation, a feeling and/or thought, which reinforces a feeling, which triggers further thought in the same vein. And so on ... (These loops can go on for a very long time unless we have good Bounce-back!)

As we practise using Power Tools like the BELL and get better at distinguishing ourselves as the author of our thoughts and feelings, rather than the victim of them, we slow things down and expand the gap between that stimulus and our automatic response to it. We start to disentangle our MERPs. We break the spiral of the stories in our mind. Victor Frankl put it perfectly:

......

'BETWEEN THE STIMULUS AND THE
RESPONSE THERE IS A SPACE. IN
THAT SPACE IS OUR POWER TO CHOOSE
OUR RESPONSE. IN OUR RESPONSE
LIES OUR GROWTH AND OUR FREEDOM.'

......

Viktor Frankl

Perhaps mindfulness might be better called choice-fulness.

Body-fulness

Another suggestion for a new word that describes being present, fully alive to what is happening now, is body-fulness. Reclaiming our whole self means reclaiming our sense of ourselves being present in our body.

The breath takes place in the body. Being aware of what is happening in the body is a good way to be more present. As we pay attention to our felt senses, what's happening in our body right now, we intentionally move our attention away from the MERPs and break the cycle. We drive ourselves sane, back to the present. We notice the autopilot thoughts and feelings and we focus back on what's real.

Asked to point to themselves, most people point to their

77

head. Everything below the neck gets relegated to the 'nether' regions in our perspective. We take our body to the gym to get it fit, just as we take our car to the mechanic. We get cross with the various bits of it that we don't like, or that don't fit with some idealized image, and blame it when it goes wrong. We are disembodied.

Being fulfilled requires not just realizing your body as a precious and necessary resource for your journey in life, but inhabiting it as a true expression of who you are. How your body is is how you are. You express yourself through and with your body.

More than that: your body sends messages to your brain that have a direct bearing on your mental–emotional state.

Right now, unwind your body. Uncross your arms and legs. Stand up. Plant each foot firmly on the ground hip-width apart. Centre your body around the vertical midline so that it's as symmetrical as possible. You may notice that you are skewed to the left or right. Raise your arms up slowly at your sides and above your head. Bring your hands together, clasping your fingers together, and release your index fingers, pointing them towards the ceiling. Stretch up and try to touch it. As you do so, notice your ribcage. See whether you can release your ribcage a little more and find more space to give a couple more centimetres to stretch up with.

Where else can you let go to stretch a little further and touch the ceiling? Notice what happens with your breathing – how you have little choice but to open up your lower abdomen in order to breathe in. Now slowly bring your arms down, paying attention to all the subtle changes that take place throughout your body as you do so. Standing still for a moment in neutral, notice how you feel – whether anything has changed in your experience of yourself. Pay attention to the subtle shifts in mood and body awareness, and where the locus of your attention sits now.

. . . . . .

BECOMING MORE PRESENT IN YOUR BODY IS THE QUICKEST, EASIEST AND MOST POWERFUL WAY TO GROUND YOURSELF, CLEAR THE CHATTER IN YOUR HEAD, AND BECOME MENTALLY AND EMOTIONALLY MORE BALANCED, AWAKE AND COHERENT.

. . . . . .

Coming alive

In order to be in touch with how we are feeling, our emotional selves, we need to be in touch with what we are feeling, the sensations in our bodies.

Emotions are what make us human. Emotions are what connect us together and drive us apart. Emotions are what we crave when we go to the movies. We go to be moved. The power of music lies, as Stravinsky observed, in its ability to bypass the intellect. It puts us in touch with a deeper sense of ourselves, something that we crave. Art is soul food.

To be fully alive as human beings, we need to embrace and master our emotionality, and to honour the intelligence of our emotions. Without emotion, we are empty shadows strutting and fretting our life upon the stage, then to be heard no more. (Sorry, Macbeth.) The stuff that brings life to life is our feelings. As the Tin Man in *The Wizard of Oz* knows, a life without heart is empty and meaningless.

Successful businesspeople know this, too. They freely admit to making important decisions based on their gut feeling. Numerous articles in the *Harvard Business Review* testify to the importance of EQ. EQ predicts future success better than IQ. Hiring managers prioritize EQ over IQ and say they would not employ someone with low EQ even if they had a high IQ.

The recent upsurge in interest in EQ testifies to the fact that we are waking up (again) to the importance of our emotionality. All the wiring for us to be EQ superstars is there from birth, but we have not learned how to use it very well. On the contrary, many experiences have caused us to doubt, damage or deny these latent abilities.

Now we need to reclaim them, and the place to start is in the body.

EQ Competence: Somatic awareness

Somatic awareness is our second EQ Competence. It's more than a physical awareness. It's a sense of oneself being present in our body.

Our ability to be in touch with the myriad of sensations and changes that are occurring moment by moment in our body, **interoception**, is directly proportional to our ability to be in touch with our feelings. Emotions are shifts in this internal milieu to which we assign meaning according to context, past experience and intention.

Are you aware of the feeling of the shower water on your skin? Do you notice when your heart starts beating faster or your gut starts churning? Do you like to spend time quietly reflecting on what's going on within you? Do you feel that other people's pain is almost tangible to you? If so, you probably have a **high somatic awareness**.

Do you tend not to pay much attention to what you are feeling? Or do you find it difficult to put that into words when you have to? Do people sometimes ask you why you're sad or angry and you think to yourself 'But I'm not!' Do you sometimes fail to notice someone else's emotional state and then get into hot water because of that? Chances are you have a **low somatic awareness**.

The science bit

The cortex is the second newest part of our brain in evolutionary terms, the newest being the prefrontal cortex (see Unit 2). Of the 100 billion nerve cells in your brain, the cortex accounts for about 40 billion of them. That's 40,000,000,000.

A part of the cortex near the front is called the **insula**. Until quite recently it wasn't clear what the insula's function was so it tended to get ignored, even though it's about 30 per cent bigger in humans than it is in other mammals. Now it's moving centre stage because of what is now recognized as its crucial role in our ability to feel our feelings and those of others – that is, our EQ and empathy.

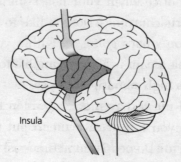

Insula

The back part of the insula, the **posterior insula**, is the receiving zone for input from the internal organs of the body, the physiological state inside us. Heart, lungs, bladder, sex organs, gut, skin – all are mapped out with their own area on the posterior insula. You've got a raised heart rate? The posterior insula notices that. You've got increased gut motility? The designated area of the posterior insula has activated that.

Now here's the really interesting bit. Signals from the posterior insula get sent through to the front part, the **anterior insula**, where meanings get assigned to those sensations. The anterior insula communicates with other parts of the brain, notably the amygdala, orbito-frontal and anterior cingulate cortex, and assigns an interpretation to those signals. The signals get interpreted and labelled as a socially significant event, an emotion.

Let's suppose that your amygdala tends to run near red alert. You anticipate, and therefore tend to experience, events as potentially threatening. Let's say your posterior insula now receives input that your heart rate has gone up. Given the context as appraised by the anterior cingulate cortex plus the red alert amygdala, the interpretation is likely to be 'Something bad is about to happen.' The raised heart rate is read as a feeling of anxiety.

Here's another scenario. It's your birthday. You feel relaxed and happy. You get breakfast in bed. Then you hear some rustling behind the bedroom door. Your heart rate goes up. In this instance, the amygdala is quiescent: the anterior cingulate is anticipating good things based on past experience.

Motto:

······

'WE DON'T
EXPERIENCE REALITY,
WE INTERPRET IT.'

······

So what's the net interpretation? 'I'm excited!' Kids burst in with presents and laughter.

In a condition called alexithymia, the insula seems not to work properly. As a result, people find it difficult to recognize physical sensations and attribute emotion. They live in a kind of emotional no-man's land that leads to relationship difficulties, social ineptitude and avoidance of people. There's no somatic awareness.

Power Tool: Breath

Your breath is a powerful tool for generating clarity, focus and wellbeing. Breathing well is essential for health and vitality. Awareness of the breath brings us back into our body, brings us into the present. Here's a picture of how breathing happens in the body.

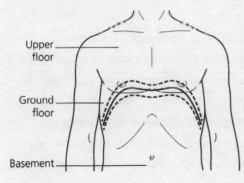

Upper floor
- Shallow breathing
- Tension
- Insufficient oxygen
- Feeling of anxiety

Ground floor
- Ribs involved
- Expansion and opening up
- Better gaseous exchange

Basement
- Diaphragm used naturally
- Nervous system balanced
- Tensions released
- More focus and presence

Notice how you are breathing right now.

Upper Floor: Put your hands on your upper chest and feel what happens as you breathe normally. When we are tense, anxious or nervous, we tend to breathe into the upper part of the chest, or even hold our breath. As this becomes our default mode, muscles stiffen up through disuse, and it can feel quite uncomfortable to breathe more deeply against this holding pattern.

Ground Floor: If you give yourself a hug around your middle, you will feel your ribs going around your sides. Now breathe in so as to push your hands away. Experiment with feeling how far down the ribs go and how far out you can make them go. This brings the breathing into the chest and more fully aerates the lungs, getting rid of more of the waste product of energy metabolism – carbon dioxide – and bringing more oxygen into your bloodstream to be carried to every cell in your body.

Basement: Place your hands on top of each other under your tummy button. As you breathe in, push your hands away from you, expanding your tummy as fully as you can. Really allow your tummy to bulge out as you breathe in. When you breathe out, squeeze out as much air as you can, imagining your tummy coming closer to your spine. Do this three or four more times. You are now utilizing your diaphragm and lung capacity more fully. You are stimulating the parasympathetic side of your ANS and vagus nerve, slowing things down and bringing greater coherence between all body systems.

Babies basement breathe. Watch their tummies go in and out when they are sleeping. As we retrain ourselves to breathe more fully, this simple act restores health, balance and vitality.

B	Body	Your breath is in your **body**.
R	Reliable	It is **reliable**, always there.
E	Effortless	It rises and falls **effortlessly**.
A	Adaptability	**Adaptability** is its nature.
T	Thankful	Its presence gives us something to be **thankful** for.
H	Healing	**Healing** happens when we breathe deeper and slower.

. . . .

WHEN IN DOUBT, FOCUS ON YOUR BREATH.
BREATHE MORE SLOWLY AND MORE
DEEPLY. FEEL WHAT HAPPENS IN YOUR
BODY. RECONNECT WITH YOUR
POWER – YOUR BREATH.

. . . .

Back to body-fulness

By spending time every day attending to the sensations in our body, as we do in mindfulness exercises, we become more attuned to sensations and more awake to our emotional state. As we increase the gap between stimulus and response, we notice the ebb and flow of feelings. We become more somatically aware.

MRI scans show that the insula increases in size with regular formal practice. The neural substrate that enables us to be in touch with ourselves expands hand in hand with our ability. As we are more able to notice and register our own feelings accurately, we develop better EQ – our ability to notice those of others improves – and better empathy.

> Feel the aliveness in your body right now. Be aware of what sensations are arising where, and follow that freely. Allow your breath to expand a little more into your tummy. Take a moment to check through from toes to head. See where you notice tension or softness in your body. See whether you can bring your awareness to areas you are not routinely conscious of, such as your armpits or the area behind you knees. Explore your body with your mind's eye and notice what you notice.

There is a recording of a full-body scan meditation available here: www.teachyourself.com/downloads.

Mindful Moment: SMS

As often as you can – and especially if you are desk bound – Stretch, Move, Sigh (SMS):

S   Stretch.   Push your arms, shoulders and chest upwards and outwards.

M   Move.   Get up. See where your body feels like it needs to move. Get in touch with where there is tension in your body. Move that bit. Free it up. Move your legs and feet.

S   Sigh.   Exhale fully. Allow the breath to escape softly over your vocal chords as your jaw drops down to allow a 'yay' to emerge, as quietly or as loudly as the circumstances permit. Squeeze out every last drop of stale air. You will then naturally inhale deeply.

Skill Set for Health: Acceptance

The Skill Set for Health theme for this unit is acceptance.

Acceptance does not mean 'giving into' or 'putting up with' – quite the opposite. Acceptance is about really, truly, getting and understanding how things are right now. It means dropping the struggle against what already is.

Acceptance means making room for things and opening

up rather than closing down – expanding *into* life, rather than contracting *against* it. Giving things some breathing space, and letting them be there, as indeed they already are, without getting caught up in them or overwhelmed by them.

The more you can give sensations, feelings and thoughts room to move, the easier it is for them to come and go without them draining you or holding you back. You are not your thoughts; you *have* thoughts. Let them be and they will let you be. To have feelings is to be human. Accept what is there and it will pass, like the weather. All things do.

Self-acceptance is the key to true growth. Don't fight against the way you are right now. Accept this fully. Learn to appreciate, validate and support who you are right now. This acceptance itself catalyses profound change.

To help you record your progress, download the *Mindfulness Playbook* Weekly Record Sheet from here: www.teachyourself.com/downloads.

Erkhart Tolle puts it well:

......

'THIS MOMENT IS AS IT SHOULD BE. WHEN YOU STRUGGLE AGAINST THIS MOMENT YOU STRUGGLE AGAINST WHAT ALREADY IS. AND WHAT'S THE SENSE IN THAT? YOU CAN WISH THINGS TO BE DIFFERENT IN THE

FUTURE BUT IN THIS MOMENT THEY ARE AS THEY ARE. THIS LEADS TO RESPONSIBILITY WHICH MEANS NOT BLAMING ANYONE OR ANYTHING FOR YOUR SITUATION, INCLUDING YOURSELF.´

······

Eckhart Tolle

What would my life look like if I started now to accept myself exactly I was? What would change? What would I get on with that I don't while I'm waiting to be better?

Homework: 'WWW?' journal

The homework for this unit is to start a 'WWW?' – What Went Well?' – journal. At the end of each day, write in your journal three things that went well that day. Scan back through the day and find three things that were fabulous, good or even just OK. Be grateful for the little things, which means looking for them. By doing this, you exercise important mental muscles and subtly shift your view of the world. Parts of your brain related to wellbeing change and grow. Chemical changes in your body improve your physical health. Keep doing this journal and return to it if life seems to pale. Now there's a challenge!

Download the *Mindfulness Playbook* 'WWW Journal' from here: www.teachyourself.com/downloads.

Daily Formal Practice

The key ingredients for success in your Daily Formal Practice are consistency and commitment. Remind yourself what your intention is. Why you are doing this? Approach your practice with passion, patience and perseverance ... and, above all, with kindness towards yourself.

Increase your sitting time if that feels right. However, two minutes' dedicated activity is more powerful than ten minutes of half-hearted sitting. Though even that is better than nothing!

UNIT 4

● ● ● ● ● ●

- **The Science Bit:** The role of the hippocampus
- **Mindful Moment:** ABC
- **Motto:** 'Conscious awareness and intention dissolve the unconscious past.'
- **EQ Competence:** Situational sensitivity
- **Power Tool:** DID – Do It Differently
- **Skill Set for Health:** Curiosity
- **Homework:** Do It Differently

••••••

Taking stock

The intellect is a powerful and useful tool, sharpened by a good education. We use our intellect to discern, discuss, understand more deeply and progress our worldview. And ... it is just one facet of our consciousness.

The first moment of perception, as a stimulus hits the brain, is non-conceptual. There is a split-second – and I do mean split-second – of pure awareness. Then the concept-making parts of the brain kick in, compare the input to our pre-existing internal model of reality, and there we have it, the interpretation of that stimulus – 'I see a cat.'

Perhaps mindful self-awareness is improving our ability to notice that interpretation quicker, so we can see more clearly the habits that construct our meaning of it, our unconscious bias. This is a very powerful use of the mind to examine itself.

Take a moment to take stock of where you are in your life. Press 'Pause': plant your feet on the ground, pull up through the spine, and soften your jaw, shoulders and eyes. Unplug. Slow down. Breathe. Allow yourself to drop down to a stiller, calmer space inside yourself. Take your time. Bring to mind a time you felt at peace or a time you felt safe, warm and loved. With an intention of kindness, ask yourself: 'Where am I in my life?' Sit with that question for a moment or two. What answers emerge from your heart or deeper within you?

Make a note of what you noticed in this box:

Untangling the knots

How are you getting on with your Daily Formal Practice? As it progresses, the knots of mental–emotional reaction patterns, our MERPs, start to loosen and slip undone. Habits that don't serve us become more apparent and, as we increase that gap between the stimulus and response, we get better at choice-fulness. Rather than being the victim of hapless circumstance, we discover how to be 'at cause', to choose, to create. Yes, circumstances can be tough but we can alter our inner landscape, which in turn alters how we greet and respond to those circumstances.

......

'HUMAN BEINGS, BY CHANGING
THE INNER ATTITUDES OF
THEIR MIND, CAN TRANSFORM
THE OUTER ASPECTS
OF THEIR LIVES.'

......

William James

One single cell in the cerebellum, the part of the brain largely responsible for this master plan of coordination, connects to more than 200,000 other nerve cells. When we learned to walk, vast arrays of neural networks co-ordinated across widely disparate parts of our brain, and wired together as we learned to balance, lift, adjust, move around obstacles, step over toys. Whole new horizons opened up to us as we gained independence from the floor and discovered freedom through the manipulation of our legs. In a healthy child, all this unfolds naturally.

Later in life, maybe you take driving lessons. Imagine the rewiring that accompanies this massive feat of learning, so that, without conscious effort, we can chat, tune the radio and make important decisions all while controlling this potentially lethal lump of metal.

We are creatures of habit. We have to be. Much of daily functioning needs to be on automatic. Habituation is what Aldous Huxley called our 'mental reducing valve'. We no longer have to pay attention. The habit goes unconscious. We are unaware.

However, among these complex unconscious habituated neural pathways are patterns that don't serve us, that clutter up our mental clarity, obscure our emotional balance and get in the way of us fulfilling our potential. This is our **subconscious script**.

All these beliefs, attitudes, patterns of behaviour and habitual ways of thinking that have built up over the years are represented in the brain by well-worn neural pathways of incredible complexity. And that's where choice-fulness comes in. Becoming aware of our habits as they emerge and as they demand that we act them out loosens the knot of the grip they have on us.

Once we notice a pattern of thought, emotional reaction or action that no longer serve us, its neural pathways are altered by the very fact that we have observed it. We have introduced the possibility of choice. As we saw before, stress, anxiety and inner turmoil are the enemies of choice. As we dial down our stress, and cultivate kindness towards ourselves, we open up the gap and allow choice to enter.

......

BECOMING AWARE OF OUR HABITS AS THEY EMERGE AND AS THEY DEMAND THAT WE ACT THEM OUT LOOSENS THE KNOT OF THE GRIP THEY HAVE ON US.

......

Motto:

······

'CONSCIOUS
AWARENESS
AND INTENTION
DISSOLVE THE
UNCONSCIOUS PAST.'

······

Breaking bad

Let's take a look at the habits you have that don't work for you. These can be:

- **repetitive thought patterns** at the back of your head like 'You idiot!', 'You can't!', 'People are so annoying', 'I'm so useless/fat/ugly/damaged/misunderstood/unappreciated.' And so on.

- **recurring emotional reactions.** The family is a great place to look for these. So is work. It's that sense of irritation that 'they' always do 'that thing'; the feeling of being unheard at dinner with your parents; the impatience that instantly arises in you when you see the toothpaste lid on the floor; the tendency to shrink inside yourself when asked a question at work; worrying about pretty much everything that hasn't happened yet.

- **behaviours that damage your wellbeing.** Bingeing on a TV box set the night before a big presentation, on a whole bar of chocolate, on digital technology or on chemicals that alter your emotional state such as alcohol, nicotine, sugar, cocaine, recreational drugs; being addicted to exercise as a way of purging stress; shouting at people; working too late; not taking enough breaks; biting your nails; being in a hurry; always pushing.

Dr Barbara Mariposa

Offload some your habits that don't serve you here.

> **HABITS THAT DON'T SERVE YOU ANY MORE**

Now write in this box some of the habits you have that work for you – for example, actions like cleaning your teeth, saying thank you, eating a healthy breakfast and nurturing good friendships, as well as thoughts like 'I'm really good at maths/caring for myself/cooking...', 'I feel loved', 'I am enough.'

> **HABITS THAT SERVE YOU**

An addiction is an autopilot reaction that has the potential to harm us and over which we have little or no control. We are all addicted to something. It's a spectrum, at the far end of which are people who get labelled addicts because there is a substance involved – such as alcohol, cocaine or nicotine – that has clear physical damaging effects on wellbeing, or because there is a compulsive behaviour such as over- or under-eating, gambling and sex.

These patterns evolve as escapes from feelings we don't want because they're uncomfortable or painful. They become well-worn paths in the brain. Following an incoming stimulus that triggers us, signals take this path of least resistance because it's easier. The addictive behaviour wraps us, albeit temporarily, in a cocoon of feeling safe. It's like a friend that understands and comforts us. It's a false friend, of course: with addictive behaviour there's always a downside.

Certain belief systems are addictive and hold us in their grip: 'I'm a failure', 'I don't belong', and 'I'm so alone.' Underneath these is the fundamental habitual thought pattern we upload early on in life: 'I'm not OK.' This single unconscious thought pattern/belief forms the background hum to many people's lives.

Once we start to untangle the invisible knots that seem to hold us so tight, we start to let go of these powerful beliefs and the stories that keep them in place. Remember:

......

'CONSCIOUS AWARENESS AND INTENTION DISSOLVE THE UNCONSCIOUS PAST.'

......

Breaking out

By practising mindful self-awareness, being present in our body, and making choices that serve us, we are rewiring our malleable brains and learning to extend that gap between stimulus and response.

And the result?

- We notice the thoughts and feelings that grab us from behind before we act them out.

- We develop better impulse control.

- We become less distractible and stay focused in line with our intention.

- We have better mastery of our feelings, are calmer and have less need to escape into the cocoon of habit.

- We develop better personal will power, rather being run by 'won't' power.

Power Tool: DID – Do It Differently

The Power Tool for Unit 4 is DID – Do It Differently. In those situations where you know habit has the upper hand, make a conscious intention to Do It Differently. Practise with the everyday things in life, like where you sit for breakfast, your journey to work, where you buy your lunch, how you spend your free time. As you reach for the chocolate biscuits, cigarettes or G&T, use one of the Mindful Moments to ground yourself back in your body and engage your CEO. In touch with your higher functioning and inner core, choose to DID.

Mindful Moment: ABC – Aware. Body. Choose.

You're in the supermarket. Your hand is reaching for that bottle of red wine, block of chocolate or, in my case, packet of biscuits. How can you, in that moment, engage your CEO and make a choice that breaks the circuit? How can you Do It Differently? Know your ABC: Aware. Body. Choose.

A. Awareness Acknowledge what's happening. Accept this moment as it is. You are in the grips of a neural pathway firing away on autopilot.

B. Body Be present in your body. And ring your BELL – Breathe. Expand. Listen. Look.

C. Choose change Engage your CEO, expand your sense of yourself and what is possible.

I'm not saying that it's easy but it is definitely doable. Again, the magic word is **intention**. What is your intention in this moment?

Take some time now to drop down below the ripples on the surface, to a deeper, quieter place. Bring your body into alignment, pull up through the spine, soften your eyes and release your jaw. Release your shoulders. Just for now let go of anything that is bothering you. Connect with your breath.

Slow your breath down a little to the count of five. Stay with that for a minute or so. Now imagine a situation that repeatedly plugs you in, gets you upset or has you react in a way that doesn't work. Whatever pops up is probably the right thing. Imagine that situation. Recreate the scenario as fully as you can. Another person's posture or voice. What are they saying? What is happening?

Go through your ABC:

A. Awareness Acknowledge and accept that this is what is happening right now.

B. Body Now see what's happening with your body and breath. How is your posture? What sensations are arising? Focus on your voice, breathing, what you are saying, how you are feeling. Now take a deep breath. Ring your BELL. – Breathe. Expand. Listen. Look. Invite a sense of warmth and appreciation into your body.

C. Choose See whether you can change your habit and DID – Do It Differently. What else is possible? What outcome would you like? What is your intention? How could you be true to yourself in this situation? Imagine yourself doing this. Notice how you feel – about yourself; about the situation and about any people involved.

Now feel your feet on the ground. Follow your breath for a minute or two. When you are ready, open your eyes, look around the room and SMS – Stretch. Move. Sigh.

EQ Competence: Situational sensitivity

Let's look at the next EQ Competence: situational sensitivity. How good are you at unconsciously tuning in to the implicit rules of social engagement in any situation and adapting accordingly?

People with **high situational sensitivity** 'get' these rules almost intuitively. They adapt, fit in, mould to the ambient mood, and unspoken rules of engagement. Some people may be over-pliable, so keen to fit in that they lose their anchor point, their own inner core, and act in ways that are not true to who they are. Their need to fit in may inhibit their own spontaneity and leave them feeling paralysed. They monitor themselves and what they say carefully, and worry about what other people think of them.

People with **low situational sensitivity** tend to be somewhat oblivious to what's going on around them, which can make them seem clumsy and inappropriate. At the extreme, they may appear dominating and unpliable, have difficulty adapting and not make good team members. They don't notice the implicit rules of social engagement and don't care that they don't. What's more, they don't care that they don't care! They may get what they want by commanding and controlling.

As human beings, it is natural, if not essential, to be responsive and adaptive, to build social cohesion and foster good relationships. A **balanced situational sensitivity** means that we stay in touch with our own inner core and with what we know to be true, and, at the same time, are appropriate and effective in how we express ourselves and behave.

Good leaders do this. They have good Bounce-back, bringing themselves back into balance with their inner core, learning more about themselves as they do so. They have strong somatic awareness, so they are in touch with how they are feeling and good at responding to what is going on around them. Their situational sensitivity allows them to fit in but not lose themselves, stay connected to self and others, and thereby be effective by influence and empathy rather than control.

The science bit: The role of the hippocampus

A part of the brain called the hippocampus has a big part to play in how we remember. It helps translate things into meaningful events and builds memories.

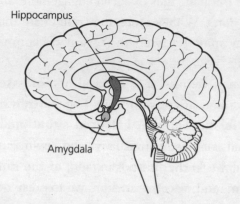

Hippocampus

Amygdala

A lot of learning happens unconsciously or implicitly. We don't realize that we are remembering stuff but somehow or other there it is. Every day you walk down the same street and past a Starbucks sign on the corner. When someone asks where the nearest Starbucks is, up pops this image, even though you have never consciously chosen to register that piece of information.

The anterior hippocampus helps regulate how we moderate our behaviour according to context, allowing us to be sensitive and appropriate. Cortisol, released in higher doses than we need when we are under chronic stress, inhibits growth of new nerve cells in the hippocampus, which affects learning and memory. In depression, the hippocampus shrinks and is less active. Our ability to be situationally sensitive decreases, making us feel clumsy and socially awkward, which can increase our sense of isolation and separateness, part of the pain of depression.

Creatures of habit

As we've seen, we don't experience reality – we interpret it through a filter of beliefs, attitudes and habits represented by neural pathways in our brain. Memory has a strong part to play in this.

When a small red-haired lady who reminds you of your old evil maths teacher pushes in front of you in the queue at the supermarket, you get unduly upset and mutter 'Silly old bag!'

That guy on the bus in a hoody pushes a memory button in your brain about a TV programme where someone who looked like that had a knife and stabbed the woman next to him. You see him through this pre-programmed filter, which may fit right in with other racial and gender stereotypes you'd uploaded earlier in life and didn't know you had. This is called unconscious bias.

......

WE DON'T EXPERIENCE REALITY – WE INTERPRET IT.

......

Nothing means anything except the meaning you give it and we are meaning-making machines.

Waking up to how we are wired, being more present,

noticing things as they are, rather than as we interpret them to be, we start to dissolve the unconscious past from our consciousness.

Skill Set for Health: Curiosity

The Skill Set for Health theme for this unit is curiosity. Have you ever watched a small child at work? They are endlessly curious, continuously exploring their physical environment: what their bodies can do, what happens if you pour water into the sock drawer, how the sieve fits over their head, the effect of a wooden spoon banging against a metal saucepan, lifting up every stone to see the worms crawl out... they are learning, wiring, expanding, growing, working hard to make sense of their world.

What happens to that wonderful sense of curiosity and unending hunger for learning? Who or what erodes it? School? Social acculturation? Grownups' voices saying 'Don't do that!', 'Don't be stupid!', 'Watch out!'? Negative experiences that hurt physically and/or emotionally? Things we are told: 'Good children sit still' 'Father Christmas won't come if you are bad'? Internalized beliefs: 'You're not creative', 'Boys shouldn't cry', 'Better the devil you know than the devil you don't', 'Best to play safe' ...?

As adults, we learn to run with the rules of our society. But where do these rules come from? Do they work? Are they conducive to our health and fulfilment and to the flourishing of an open, accepting and compassionate society? To what extent has who you perceive yourself to be been shaped by the invisible forces of sociocultural determinants around gender, race, age, status, IQ, educational attainment?

Where and how do you limit yourself? What do your chattering monkeys tell you about yourself, others and the world? How much of all of that is actually true?

Be curious. Explore the world with new eyes each day. What do the buildings around you look like? Can you see something new on your way to work every day? Who is that person you see every day? What thoughts, feelings and actions expand your sense of who you are, and which of them don't? Which ones drain you of energy and which ones feed your energy supply, your inner battery?

To help you record your progress, download the *Mindfulness Playbook* Weekly Record Sheet from here: www.teachyourself.com/downloads.

......

CURIOSITY IS THE BOAT THAT SETS US
FREE ON THE OCEAN OF OUR
OWN IMAGININGS AND POSSIBILITIES,
AND UNLOCKS THE BELIEF BOXES WE
LIVE IN THAT KEEP US ON THE SHORE.

......

Homework: Doing It Differently

The homework for this unit is DID – Do It Differently.

You can intentionally create neural pathways in your brain by choosing to DID – Do It Differently. Turn left out of the front door instead of right. Find a new way to walk to the station. Sit in a different place at breakfast. Rearrange your desk. Novelty is an aphrodisiac for your brain. It wakes up key areas and releases the BDNF (Brain-Derived Neurogenic Factor), promoting the growth of new neural highways.

When you are going into that awkward meeting, be aware of what you are predicting will happen, based on the past. Ask yourself what you can do differently. How can you use the BELL, ABC and DID, to put you in touch with your Expanded Self rather than your Small Self? What outcome do you wish for? What is your intention? Engage CEO functioning before Neighbourhood Watch takes over. Take a moment to readjust and reset if it already has.

Download the *Mindfulness Playbook* 'Doing It Differently' Record Sheet from here: www.teachyourself.com/downloads.

Daily Formal Practice

Some days we would really rather stay in bed than get up and just 'sit' there. The gravitational pull of this resistance makes the body feel heavier, as we snuggle further down under the duvet. Or is it a 'don't-vet'?

These are the times when you need to gird your loins and 'just do it', because you said you would and because you are worth it! Do It Differently.

Those chattering monkeys just want to show us who's boss and pull us back into old habits, 'There you are – I knew you couldn't.' When we keep our word to ourselves in the face of these cheeky monkeys, we find out who we really are. We strengthen ourselves against the forces of our own patterns and get up and do it anyway. Because you said you would. It's all about self-discipline!

The feeling you get when you do this, when you win against the chattering monkeys, is amazing. Integrity rules. You feel good about yourself. You have weakened the links in the memory chain, the 'I'm not OK' patterns that keep you stuck.

Make your word law in the universe. Keep your word to yourself, even when no one is watching. This is integrity, wholeness, health.

······

'WE DON'T BREAK THE RULES; WE BREAK OURSELVES AGAINST THE RULES.'

······

Cecil B. DeMille

UNIT 5

• • • • • •

- **The Science Bit:** The fusiform gyrus
- **Mindful Moment:** Kindness starts with you
- **Motto:** 'Health is other people.'
- **EQ Competence:** Non-verbal intuition
- **Power Tool:** AEIOU
- **Skill Set for Health:** Learning
- **Homework:** Labels

••••••

Doing what comes naturally

Humans are social animals. We need one another and we need to be needed. Social isolation is a risk factor in heart disease along with obesity and smoking. Ninety per cent of the brain cells in the cerebral cortex are devoted to processing information about social interaction.

Emotions are intelligent. They contain vital information about what's going on within and around us. **Emotional intelligence** is our birth right. We are born with all the equipment in place to be emotionally intelligent. By this I mean the ability to read, interpret and translate our own feelings and those of others, and respond appropriately and effectively.

A fundamental ingredient in this is our **somatic awareness** (see Unit 3), the ability to be in touch with, and responsive to, the sensations that arise in our bodies, and the sense we have of ourselves being present in our bodies, of being embodied.

How do you trust your self? How much importance do you give to your 'gut' feelings, your instinct, your intuition? How good are you at interpreting the signs accurately?

119

Since Renaissance times our sense of self has shifted upwards to the head, to the brain and to the powers of reason. The assumption is made that consciousness and reason are one and the same, but they aren't.

In this upwards migration, we have lost touch with our embodied self, the sense of being whole and complete, connected and belonging. Stuck in our heads, it is difficult to feel that sense of belonging and connectedness that most of us crave.

......

TO BE EMOTIONALLY INTELLIGENT IS TO RECLAIM OUR AWARENESS OF OURSELVES IN OUR BODIES, REDISTRIBUTE THE POWER FROM HEAD TO WHOLE PERSON, AND LEARN AGAIN TO TRUST THE INNATE SKILLS WE WERE BORN WITH.

......

All you need is love

Vast amounts of learning take place in the first two years of life. The basis of our EQ is laid down in the neural pathways that develop in the early years. Love, safety, caring touch and responsive relating lead to successful software being installed in the emotional hardware we are born with. This allows us to grow into secure, well-balanced, adaptive adults who build strong bonds with the right people with integrity and authenticity. In touch with who we are, we trust our instincts, listen to our gut and have a good balance between reason and intuition.

Life seldom proceeds down this rosy path the way we would like. Parents are humans too, with their own patterns, inadequacies and inner battles. Children pick up on the ambient emotional tone within the home. As we've seen, when the amygdala is triggered, emotional intelligence goes out of the window. To grow straight and strong, children need love, safety and a sense of being seen for who they are.

Luckily, all the essential wiring for healthy emotional functioning is always there, except in extreme cases, *despite* any faulty software that might get uploaded earlier in life. And the brain is plastic: it changes shape according to how we use it.

The ability to regain a sense of love, being loved and being loving has huge healing potential. By cultivating kindness and compassion towards ourselves and others, we become our own source of love. We can nurture the habits that encourage growth. Generosity, acceptance, appreciation and curiosity all provide rich soil for healthy growth and are wonderful energy feeders.

Motto:

......

'HEALTH IS OTHER
PEOPLE.'

......

Where does 'I' live?

Our Daily Formal Practice encourages us to deepen our breathing, dialling up the parasympathetic side of the ANS, and shifting our physiological state towards greater coherence. It also helps us dial down the grip of those cheeky chattering monkey thoughts. Thoughts are events, electrochemical activity in the brain. Let them be, accept them as they are without judgement, and they will let you be.

So ... if we are not our thoughts, who are we?

Here's a useful set of questions to engage your mind with:

• What is happening right now?

• To whom is it happening? Who is noticing that?

• Where does the 'I' that is doing the noticing and focusing live?

• What is the source of the intention that moves the focus of your attention from thought to breath? From chattering monkeys to expanded self-awareness? Who is creating the thoughts? What if the source of all that arises, this Expanded Self, was inherently whole, complete and loving?

Just a thought ... When I started down the Zen path, the sensei would say things that, to be honest, meant very little to me. He would say 'When the sun gets up in the morning you can either laugh or cry. The sun doesn't care', and my mind would retort: 'Well, that's not very nice of it, is it?' After some time, I realized that it doesn't *not* care either. It just is.

The world keeps turning, spring passes into summer, the river and its ripples are constantly impermanent. What I make of all this is up to me. Life throws us challenges and difficulties. What I make them mean can add another layer of pain – secondary suffering – or it may not. Someone treads on my foot. It hurts. Then I add to that with the mental–emotional reaction patterns (MERPs) that pile in. 'That idiot! Now I won't be able to go dancing! What if it's broken?' and so on.

......

THE FIRST ARROW OF SUFFERING IS INEVITABLE. THE SECOND ARROW, THE ONE WE THROW AT OURSELVES, IS OPTIONAL.

......

Buddha

EQ Competence: Non-verbal intuition

When we cultivate stillness within ourselves, we allow the voice of our inner wisdom to be heard. We seem to remember what we already know.

Part of that wisdom is the ability to 'know' what is going on with other people. Thanks to our innate abilities to be emotionally intelligent, we sense when someone is lying to us, feeling happy, comfortable with themselves, hiding something or at ease within a conversation.

This ability is the fourth EQ Competence: non-verbal intuition

We've all been in situations when we feel something isn't right but we can't quite put our finger on what it is. Our inner radar is alerted. We are picking up signals that our rational mind can't make sense of. Do we trust this or let our heads tell us to pull ourselves together and get a grip?

In order to trust our non-verbal intuition, we need to be well grounded in our bodies – to have somatic awareness – so that we can notice the subtle cues and changes in our own physiology. We need to have a strong inner core and be able to bounce back to this inner core when something throws us off balance, so we can notice the signs around us and in us, and register them accurately. We need, in short, self-awareness.

The ability to read body language, tone of voice and facial expression is fundamental to successful social interaction. We are constantly reading the delicate dance of minute super-fast and fleeting micro-expressions together with subtle shifts in voice, posture, muscle tension, emotion and meaning.

The more present we are, the more accurate we are in noticing and responding to this continuous dance. The clearer we are in ourselves, the more anchored we are in our inner core, the better able we are to gauge what's going on with other people and respond appropriately and effectively.

The science bit: The fusiform gyrus

The visual cortex sits towards the back of the brain. Within it lies a specialized area called the fusiform gyrus that deals with information about the face, recognizing faces, noticing expressions and relaying information to higher centres.

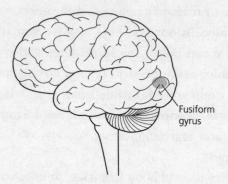

Fusiform
gyrus

Humans are the only mammals to have white sclera, the bit surrounding the dark hole in the middle of the eye, the pupil. Other primates have brown sclera. The white sclera creates sharp contrast so we can notice minute changes in pupil size and gaze direction, and 'read' the mind behind those eyes. In other primates, the dark sclera obscures this important information from its prey and thus has a clear survival advantage.

People who are towards the bottom end of a spectrum passing through Asperger's to autism have difficulty making or maintaining eye contact. What happens when they do make eye connect is fascinating. It seems that it provokes huge anxiety. Activity in the amygdala is markedly increased. Rather that their poor eye contact being due to some deficit in the fusiform gyrus, as was previously thought, it's the anxiety that such eye contact provokes that causes them to look away and avoid this pivotal human behaviour.

As a result, such people miss out on vast chunks of vital information about other people, their emotional state and their true intentions, which in turn makes it difficult for them to respond appropriately, feel connected, fit in socially or experience empathy.

Where would you place yourself with regard to non-verbal intuition? Where would those who know you well place you?

Write down your answers here:

MY NON-VERBAL INTUITION

What about the people in your life? How much of their behaviour could be attributed to where they lie on the situational sensitivity and non-verbal intuition scales?

OTHER PEOPLE'S NON-VERBAL INTUITION

You know those times when we're talking with someone and know they're not really listening yet we carry on talking anyway. What stops us from politely and discreetly flagging this rather than carrying on the charade of non-communication? When you are the one that's drifted off to think about what you're having for tea, do you pretend to have heard it all, or gently say, 'Really sorry, I lost you there for a moment. Could you say that again, please?'

Just as we notice all the subtle signs, so do others. Nothing is hidden actually. The more embodied and present we are the easier it is to stay true to ourselves.

Eye contact has another important function. Oxytocin is a hormone released by the hypothalamus in a variety of different circumstances. In childbirth, it helps the womb contract. After birth, the mother's system is flooded with oxytocin for another reason, to promote a feeling of love, connectedness and caring between mother and baby, a bond that helps many a parent survive through the long sleepless nights of early parenthood.

Oxytocin is released when we make non-threatening eye contact with others. We need this. It feeds our sense of belonging and connectedness, which, as we have seen, are vital to wellbeing. Growing up, we need to be seen, receive love through our parents' gaze, and feel that oxytocin buzz pass between us in the process.

Non verbal intuition relies on the subliminal reading of many signals, among which eye contact and facial expression are key in human interaction.

......

PEOPLE WITH HIGH EQ TRUST THEIR NON-VERBAL INTUITION AND IN SO DOING, MAKE FEWER ERRORS OF JUDGEMENT, ARE LESS PRONE TO UNCONSCIOUS BIAS, READ SITUATIONS ACCURATELY, AND RESPOND APPROPRIATELY AND EFFECTIVELY.

......

In it together

We've talked a lot about thoughts. Now we're going to focus more on feelings. What are all those signals we are reading with our non-verbal intuition telling us? Mostly, they are calling us to recognize how others are feeling, and helping us discern whether their words match their meaning and expressed intent, and to feel what is in their heart. What lies beneath? Is this person authentic? Are all the messages I'm receiving coherent? If not, what is astray? How do I respond to that?

Beyond survival value, non-verbal intuition combines

with the other components of EQ to make us clear, effective and authentic communicators, both great listeners and powerful message senders.

Interestingly, it seems that there is a universal language of emotions that is understood across culture, social grouping and environmental influence. Wherever you are in the world, certain facial expressions will be universally interpreted as happiness or joy. Disgust will be expressed the same way in New York as in Papua New Guinea, where Paul Ekman, the man who has done so much of the groundwork in this area, did field research.

What Paul Ekman concluded was that there are six basic emotional 'calling cards'. These are joy, anger, sadness, fear, disgust and surprise. These calling cards can give rise to more subtle subsets – for example fearful anger or angry sadness. Fear may express itself angrily or anxiously.

We can use these basic six as the substrate for getting better at recognizing our own emotional state. One of the key learning opportunities in improving EQ is to recognize and label what we are feeling accurately. First we need to read ourselves – 'Uh-oh, heart beat rising, palms sweaty!' Then we need to interpret that – 'I'm feeling anxious.' Finally, we need to translate that into appropriate and effective action: 'Please may I have a hug.' So:

- Read = Notice a shift in physiological state.
- Interpret = Identify and label that.
- Translate = Take action in an appropriate and effective way.

Improving our own literacy enables us to respond more appropriately and effectively to others. We read: 'I sense tension rising. I can see it in their jaw.' We interpret it accurately: 'They're angry.' We translate this into appropriate and effective action. 'Give them their scooter back.'

It's helpful to have a rich lexicon of words to describe feelings. Often, we take the easy route and say 'I'm so stressed!' Stress is a physiological state, not an emotion. Often, there are many and conflicting feelings going on. If we can get clearer about what these are and label them, we are moving closer to being able to find their trigger and therefore the solution. 'The bus is late. I feel tension mounting in my tummy. I'm anxious. Ah, amygdala on red alert. What actions will help me feel safe again? Ah yes, the Power Tool BELL and the Mindful Moment ABC.' Job done.

Power Tool: AEIOU

Here's a simple way to drive yourself sane in the heat of emotional upheaval. It's an expanded version of the ABC tool we learned in Unit 5.

A **Awareness and Acceptance** Notice you are upset. Ring your BELL to get present.

E **Embody the experience** What can you feel in your body right now? Describe that to yourself.

I **Interpretation** What meaning are you adding to these feelings? What thoughts are arising?

O **Open up your options** What are my options right now? Engage your CEO. Widen the gap between stimulus and response and invoke choice.

U **You** Who do you choose to be in this moment? What is your intention? Are you being Small Self on autopilot or Expanded Self in touch with who you are? You choose.

Skill Set for Health: Learning

The Skill Set for Health theme for this unit is learning. As the saying goes, 'The mind is like a parachute. It works best when it's open.' All too often we shut down and assume that a particular set of events will invariably lead to the predictable consequence. We create the outcome with our belief. We generate the future based on the past.

A big job interview is coming up. You got through the two initial rounds, so you must be doing something right. No matter. Now the moment is upon you. Stress = autopilot. Subconscious script is kicking in. Default mode. The chattering monkeys are saying, 'They're going to see right through you. You're a fraud. You know you can't do this job. Your nerves always get the better of you anyway. It's over. No chance.' Use the AEIOU Power Tool:

A   **Aware**   Ring your BELL and bring yourself back to the present.

E   **Embody**   Notice what is happening in your body. Check in with something real. Embody your experience.

I   **Interpretation**   Notice what the chattering monkeys are saying, the interpretation you are adding. Let that be. You are not your thoughts.

O   **Options**   Stay open: 'What can I learn here?' Be curious: 'How could I DID – Do It Differently?'

U   **You**   'Whom do I choose to be in this moment? Small Self or Expanded Self? How could a learning approach move me forward out of my habit?'

We have the potential to learn throughout life. That road sign featuring old bent-over people is a cultural construct. It's all in the attitude. When asked how he felt about growing older, Fritz Perls replied. 'Older and growing, my dear, older and growing.' Quite.

The brain keeps on changing shape according to how you use it, so use it well. Learn a new word every day. Create a new habit that enhances your wellbeing, like the 'WWW?' journal.

......
— NOVELTY IS AN APHRODISIAC FOR THE BRAIN.
......

What can you learn about yourself today? How might another person be growing and changing? What actions and attitudes enhance learning and where do you put your attention? First create the intention and then the rest will follow.

To help you record your progress, download the *Mindfulness Playbook* 'Learning' Record Sheet from here: www.teachyourself.com/downloads.

Homework: Labels

The homework for this unit is to label the kinds of thoughts and feeling you are having. Let's look at each in turn.

THOUGHTS
Thoughts seem to fall into some pretty predicable categories. See which ones you specialize in and count how many thoughts of a particular kind you can notice in a day.

Here are some of my favourites:

• **Self-pitying:** 'Poor me', 'It's not fair.'

- **Blaming:** 'It's all their fault, the weather's fault, my parents' fault, my job's fault, money's fault.'

- **Guilt-ridden:** 'It's my fault, I deserve it, no wonder the washing machine broke!', 'What a bad person I am – I had it coming to me.'

- **Self-critical:** 'You're such a ...', 'You're too ...', You're not ... enough.'

- **Judging:** 'They are so stupid/inconsiderate/selfish/rude. She's so ...'

- **Resentful:** 'If only they hadn't ...', 'If only I had ...', 'It's not fair that ...'

- **Shameful:** 'If they knew that about me...', 'I hope they don't find out about ...'

- **Superior:** 'I know best. They know nothing! What idiots!'

Write your own here:

THOUGHT LABELS

Now that you've been doing the Daily Formal Practice for a while – you have, haven't you? – you're probably noticing some familiar friends among your chattering monkeys. You create space for your thought trains, notice them as they chug along down the track and learn how to refocus and hop off, rather than stay on board. Noticing and Focusing. Embodying and Choosing.

Start to distinguish not only that you have thoughts but also what kinds of thoughts you specialize in churning out. You may notice that one particular thought can trigger a whole chain reaction. Or recur on repeat like a stuck record. Labelling is a powerful exercise in self-awareness and leads us to greater self-knowledge and self-mastery.

It takes great mental effort to tear ourselves away from

some thoughts because they feel so familiar to us and fit so well with our Small Self image, like a well-worn shoe. They're really sticky like that kind of grass seed that gets stuck in your jumper when you're out on a walk. How can you tear yourself away to be present in the midst of a mind attack of one of your core belief patterns? When you do, the feeling of freedom is immense.

Ultimately, the final layer to peel yourself away from is that basic addiction to the thought train that says there is something wrong with you. It takes courage to give up that addiction!

I remember lying in bed shortly after my 60th birthday. A particularly pernicious, self-undermining train of thought was chugging away. 'Well, Barbara, you're retirement age now. You can take it easy. Look at those wrinkles. Just be happy you have three kids so when *they* have children you'll have a part to play as Grandma. Given the mess you've made of your life, you're lucky to have that.' And so on. It all felt very real and made perfect sense.

A chink of light was all it took. A moment of self-recognition. I saw the train, jumped off and let it roll on by, disentangling myself from this particularly sticky and familiar line of thought. I got up, brushed my teeth and sat down to start work on what became the Mind Mood Mastery programme.

FEELINGS

What are you feeling right now? Aim to put a word to it. Identify the background hum that is the emotional backdrop to your daily life. As you go about your life, ask yourself, 'What am I feeling right now?' When you get stressed, be curious and dissect it a little. What feelings got you there? What's going on now? Embody the experience. Put a label on the feeling. Become familiar with the background emotional hum that is your norm.

Here are some words to get you started: annoyed/lonely/content/shy. Add to this and build your own lexicon.

Download the *Mindfulness Playbook* 'Feeling Words' Record Sheet from here: www.teachyourself.com/downloads.

FEELING LABELS

Notice which feeling words seem to recur. What does this tell you about your habitual emotional landscape? How can you get better at recognizing, labelling and accepting what you are feeling?

Pick a word on the list and see whether you can evoke that feeling in yourself, then make it disappear again. Experiment with being at cause of your feelings, rather than at the effect of them. Which feeling words do you veer away from? Which ones attract you? How would you like to feel?

Daily Formal Practice

Infuse your Daily Formal Practice and Mindful Moments with kindness. Allow judgemental thoughts to settle. Let them be and they will let you be. Have the intention to cultivate kindness in your actions and your attitude and where you choose to put your attention. Think about the people you care about in your life. Extend kindness to them. Recognize that you, too, are human and worthy of kindness. As you would a best friend, extend the hand of kindness to yourself.

UNIT 6

• • • • • •

- **The Science Bit:** The left prefrontal cortex
- **Mindfulness:** Intention
- **Mindful Moment:** 1, 2, 3
- **Motto:** 'Get the "being" right and right "doing" will follow.'
- **EQ Competence:** Disposition
- **Power Tool:** MCM – Mess up. Clean up. Move on.
- **Skill Set for Health:** Forgiveness
- **Homework:** Forgiveness letter

••••••

Zen and the art of kitchen maintenance

The human being is perfectly designed to work best when exhibiting the behaviours and qualities that advance social cohesion. Health is other people. In this playbook we're exploring some of these ways of being, including being generous, appreciative, accepting, curious, kind and open to learning.

Sometimes, however, we just don't feel that way. It takes consciousness and intention to create your life on a daily basis. And, by its very nature, energy tends towards entropy, a gradual decline into disorder. This is the second law of thermodynamics.

I call it 'Zen and the Art of Kitchen Maintenance'. You wash all the dishes, put everything away, fold the tea towels and hang them up straight, polish the draining board and walk out with a proud final glance backwards at your handiwork.

What's the next thing to happen? Someone comes and puts their dirty dishes in the sink, leaves the coffee jar out, or uses the towel and stuffs it back over the rail, all crumpled.

This is life. Entropy. The thing is, conscious awareness

has to be reapplied afresh in every instant. We have to keep tidying the kitchen. It's the same with intention. What is my intention in this moment now? How am I being me? Who am I being?

As we do our Daily Formal Practice and use the Mindful Moments, we are building up the muscles to consciously create our experience. 'Who am I?' becomes not a place to get to or something to find, but a creative act in this moment. 'Who I am' is who I choose to be, not driven by my past and what seems probable based on my story, my narrative, but generated by my sense of what is possible moving into the future. It's laying the track down in front of the train.

Intention

As we've discussed, behind all our actions, attitudes and where we place our attention lies an intention.

ATTENTION

INTENTION ⟶ ACTION

ATTITUDE

Intention is a bit hard to define. Even the dictionary definition is tautological. In the field of logic it is defined as 'conceptions formed by directing the mind towards an object'. The key word here is direction. Intention *directs*.

······

WITH OUR INTENTION WE DRAW THE FUTURE TOWARDS OURSELVES.

······

Right now, become aware of your left big toe. Direct the spotlight of your attention fully on to your left big toe. Keep it there. Feel the aliveness in your left big toe. Imagine the bone inside it. Feel the blood pulsating through it. Now move that spotlight of attention to your right thumb. What does your right thumb feel like right now? What is it touching? Imagine the bones inside it. Feel the aliveness in your right thumb. Feel the blood pulsating through it. Now return your attention to a general awareness of what is going on around you

Now consider how you did that. How did you move your attention from toe to thumb? That was the power of your intention. Whatever you focus on gets bigger. As the adage goes, 'Energy flows where your attention goes.'

When you speak with your kids or co-workers about something important, first generate a clear intention of what you want the outcome to be. Your intention translates into your attitude and how you act, and where you put your attention. It communicates itself powerfully and, more than the words you use, is what people respond to. If your intention is subliminally destructive or unclear, this will come across. If your intention is win–win, this too will communicate itself clearly.

When you're not clear what your intention is, unconscious patterns emerge that can distort the message. Your message loses impact. Like those old radios where you turned a dial to tune in, lack of intention is like picking up the static and mixed signals from different radio stations as you twiddle the dial. Clear intention broadcasts loud and clear. You're tuned in and on message, and all with minimal effort.

There is always an intention. Often, it's unconscious. We are not aware of it. We can see it retrospectively. Intention is that sense of being purposeful which lies behind and gives meaning to all that follows. In Unit 1 we asked, 'What is my intention in sitting mindfully every day? Why am I doing it?' Integrity depends on being clear about our intentions and then lining up our actions to be true to that.

Intention can be a powerful force that aligns us around a central point, bringing head, heart, spirit and energy into alignment, generating personal power and effective action. When intention is unconscious, or when we are not aware of our intentions, a lot of energy dribbles out of the system. A kind of psychic chaos rules. There is a lack of clarity and direction.

As we get better at noticing our thoughts and feelings, we get clearer in our intention, and therefore in our actions, attitudes and where we place our attention. Energy leaks are plugged. Choice emerges.

EQ Competence: Disposition

The fifth EQ Competence is disposition. How are you oriented towards the world? What is your disposition towards it? Do you welcome new opportunities such as moving to a new city or meeting new people, imagining the friendships and possibility that might emerge? Do you see the future as better than the past? Do you look forward to a night out, and love every moment when it arrives? Do you feel energized at the end of a busy day doing the things you love? Chances are you're an **approacher** on the **disposition scale**.

Do you tend to avoid situations where you're not sure of the outcome and prefer to stick to who and what you know? Does a pleasant unexpected event give you a warm feeling for a short while, which quickly fades to your normal set point mood-wise? Do you find yourself bored by things like a beautiful sunset or playing with a small child? Does something kick in that says 'OK. Enough. This isn't it?' You're probably an **avoider** on the disposition scale.

People on the higher end of the disposition spectrum would probably be labelled optimists, those at the lower end, pessimists. There is no right or wrong with this. And

Motto:

. . . . . .

'GET THE "BEING"
RIGHT AND RIGHT
"DOING" WILL
FOLLOW.'

. . . . . .

labels are not reality. Extreme optimists can tend to bounce over the surface of life, almost refusing to see the dangers and pitfalls, or learn from their mistakes. Pessimists are shown to have a more realistic grasp of situations because they look at things more closely and make more considered choices.

And some people, when asked if they are 'glass half empty' or 'glass half full' people, will see it completely differently and answer that their glass is bigger or altogether more beautiful than anyone else's and that's what matters.

Yet there is something to be said for moving our set point up the disposition scale towards the approacher end, as we will see.

The science bit

A tendency towards pessimism correlates with being at the lower end of the disposition scale – having a tendency to avoid, withdraw, pull back – while optimism correlates with being higher on the scale – tending to approach, move towards, say 'yes'.

Let's look at an experiment. Divide a bunch of people into pessimists and optimists, rating them by energy levels, outlook on life, self-esteem, motivation, these kind of things. Now hook them up to machines that measure brain activity and show them a bunch of funny cartoons. I know, why would anyone want to do that?

Here's the thing. What you would see is that, as people

were having fun and laughing, two areas of the brain that form part of the reward centre – the nucleus accumbens and the ventral striatum – light up. These release dopamine, the 'good times' neurotransmitter. Part of the prefrontal cortex connected to these areas will also light up.

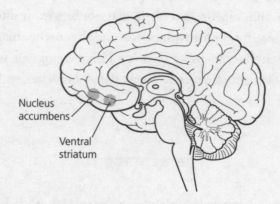

Nucleus accumbens

Ventral striatum

In approachers (those high on the disposition scale), a reverberating circuit of anticipation to have a good time sets up, so the next thing to come along creates even more excitement. The signals get amplified. It's like watching a stand-up comic. To begin with we are hesitant, unsure whether she will make us laugh or not. They do. We are reassured, start to relax, get into it, and by the end all they have to do is raise an eyebrow and we are rolling in the aisles. The circuitry becomes self-generative. 'I anticipate that I will have a good time, so I do, and then I have an even better time.' And so on.

In the other group, the avoiders, the two areas of the reward centre light up to begin with but the signal is not sustained. There's no reverb. It's as if the 'good time' signal dribbles away. 'Just because I'm having a good time now doesn't mean I'll carry on feeling good.' This is what happens in depression. Any experience of happiness is not sustained, and this may then lead to common depressive mental–emotional reaction patterns that perpetuate the feelings of inadequacy and low self-esteem. 'Everyone else is having a good time. What's wrong with me that I can't keep it up? It's all my fault.' I know this because I've been there.

Approachers tend have more activity in the left side of the prefrontal cortex (LPFC) than avoiders. In other words, optimism, motivation and 'can do'/'approach' attitude to life correlate with more activity in the LPFC than in the right side of the prefrontal cortex (RPFC). Depression, withdrawal and an avoidance outlook are characterized by greater activity in the RPFC than in the LPFC.

Now here comes the really fascinating bit. People who meditate develop more activity and more brain tissue in the LPFC. In other words, we can shift our set point towards the left. Some Buddhist monks who may have clocked up an incredible 10,000-plus hours in meditation, have up to three thousand times more activity in their LPFC than in their RPFC. They exist in a state of tranquillity, joy and wellbeing.

In addition, in other experiments it was shown that approachers produce greater quantities of antibodies in response to being given the flu virus (antigen) than avoiders.

In other words, the way you feel about yourself is related to how certain bits of your brain work, and the way your brain works affects the functioning of your immune system. Mind, emotion and body – they're all connected.

This must surely make you want to go and meditate with even greater passion, patience and perseverance!

......

YOU HAVE THE POWER WITH YOUR THOUGHT ALONE TO ALTER THE SUBSTRATE OF YOUR BRAIN IN A WAY THAT DIRECTLY ENHANCES YOUR MENTAL, EMOTIONAL AND PHYSICAL HEALTH.

......

The obstacles

The main reasons we don't follow through and do what we said we would, and what we know works, fall into three simple categories:

1. **We are lazy** – which is basically a lack of self-discipline and letting the chattering monkeys run the show.
2. **We think we're too busy** – the paradox here is self-evident.

3. We feel disheartened – in a quick-fix world we want instant results.

The unfortunate fact is that anything worth pursuing takes practice. With your Daily Formal Practice you are building self-discipline muscles that will stand you in great stead elsewhere in your life. Surprise yourself and your chattering monkeys by being the person who does what they said they would, even when no one is looking.

Take a step back and gain perspective. Press 'Pause'. One of the annual goals a businessman set himself was to spend more time with his son. He realized how addicted to busyness he was when he was relieved to find a bedtime story for his son that took only one minute to tell. That realization shocked him! Slow down and smell the roses. This is it. Now.

......

HOW YOU LIVE IN THIS MOMENT IS HOW YOU LIVE YOUR LIFE.

......

Mindful Moment: 1, 2, 3

This Mindful Moment is about getting things done, doing the things we know we have to do, and actually deep down want to do, but somehow avoid, put off or deny, fibbing to ourselves about their importance, significance or impact.

We have to be in the right state of 'being' first. Then the right 'doing' will follow. So:

1. Connect with your **self**: Focus your breathing on the area of your heart. Imagine your breath flowing into and out of your heart, slowing it and deepening it in a way that feels comfortable.

2. Connect with your **power source**: Evoke a positive sense of appreciation or care for something or someone. Breathe this in with each breath. Allow it to pervade your whole inner space.

3. Connect with your **intention**: What is the driving force, the bigger picture, the purpose? Remind yourself of this.

In short, connect to your ...

1. self
2. power source
3. intention

Connect with these and you will do the things that you know in your heart are the right things to do. Right action will follow like day follows night.

......

GET THE BEING RIGHT AND RIGHT DOING WILL FOLLOW.

......

Skill Set for Health: Forgiveness

The Skill Set for Health theme for this unit is forgiveness. Forgiveness means letting go of resentment, anger and bitterness towards people who we feel have wronged or harmed us. This includes ourselves. It is a willing change of heart that releases space in our mental–emotional life.

......

'NOT FORGIVING IS LIKE DRINKING POISON AND EXPECTING THE OTHER PERSON TO DIE.'

......

Anonymous

Forgiveness is an act of kindness to ourselves, allowing us to heal and move on, rather than keep dragging the past with us. We gain ownership of our life rather than endlessly making someone else responsible for our pain.

You miss a day in your Daily Formal Practice, feel bad and

berate yourself. You enter a vicious cycle of diminishing self-worth, so you don't bother the next day either. Don't do this! Forgive yourself and start again. Nothing got broken.

Forgiveness is ultimately a way of being. If you feel you are not ready to forgive someone, simply live with the idea of that and approach it gently and slowly. Forgiveness brings with it an incredible lightness of being, a release and sense of freedom. Those people whom we haven't forgiven have an invisible hold over us. As we hold on to blame, judgement, self-righteousness, we give them our power.

And yes, what they did may well be very wrong. To forgive is not to excuse anything, or say it was right, or to 'let them off the hook'. It's personal work we do to free ourselves from dragging that burden around with us.

The person concerned may have violated a standard you hold dear. As you become less judgemental of yourself, you might find you become less judgemental of others. They go hand in hand. Rather than avoiding the things that make you feel uncomfortable, practise approaching them instead. Exercise your LPFC. Get in touch with your higher 'noble' goals and sense of values, your Expanded Self. Who do you choose to be in this moment?

We saw in Unit 3 that as we practise mindfulness, the insula gets bigger. We become more able to be in touch with what we are feeling in our bodies and therefore with our emotions. In this way, we become more able to be aware of what others are feeling, and our ability for empathy increases. As we put ourselves in the shoes of our perpetrators, we may start to see things differently and unstick some of the firmly held beliefs that make it hard to forgive.

To help you record your progress, download the *Mindfulness Playbook* 'Forgiveness' Record Sheet from here: www.teachyourself.com/downloads.

Homework: Forgiveness letter

The homework for this unit is to write a letter of forgiveness to someone. This letter is just for you. State what they did in your eyes and what you are forgiving them for. You don't have to send this. It's an inner personal exercise to help you release some of the energy stored up in the story you carry around with you. In so doing, you allow yourself to lighten up and to heal. As we discussed, it helps to add empathy into the mix. Take a look at the situation from a broader perspective. Try to see it from their point of view, given the way their lives have been. Walk for a mile in their moccasins, as the Native American proverb has it.

If this feels like a step too far, that's fine. Simply allow the word 'forgiveness' to be present in your awareness as you go about your day. That is in itself a powerful thing. As with all the Skill Set for Health themes, just allowing the word of the theme to permeate your consciousness can shift the way you see the world. It's not about doing, it's about being. Soften the pressure you put on yourself. Remember: 'Get the "being" right and right "doing" will follow.'

•••••
ABOVE ALL, FORGIVE YOURSELF.
•••••

Power Tool: MCM – Mess up. Clean up. Move on.

The Power Tool for this unit is: Mess up. Clean up. Move on. – or MCM. In other words, self-forgiveness. Making mistakes is part of life. We limit ourselves with our fear of getting it wrong, failing, messing up. Fear of failure is a huge part of our subconscious script.

Mistakes are inevitable and an essential opportunity to learn. We also learn a huge amount when things go well. The key question is how do you deal with mistakes? Do you judge yourself, ruminate, avoid and shut down? Or do you approach, learn and expand? Acknowledge and accept that what happened happened. Because it did. Look and see what is in your heart and do what you know is the right thing to do to rectify the situation, if anything. Sometimes mistakes are imaginary!

- **Acknowledge** what happened. See it as accurately as you can. Remove the self-pity and the 'story'.
- **Accept** this fully. The past is in the past.

- **Approach** the situation rather than avoid the situation.
- **Act.** Be in action. Do something. Anything. Move
  yourself forward in whatever small way you can.
  Let it go.

The future is unwritten. We create it with our choices
in this moment. As you increase the gap between stimulus
and response and become more intentional in your action,
attitudes and where you put your attention, you create a
future that better suits who you are and that is true to your
integrity.

The traditional Hawaiian community recognizes the
importance of forgiveness for the community as a whole.
They have a beautiful communal ritual that includes the
phrase *ho'oponopono*. This has been roughly translated as:
'I'm sorry. Please forgive me. Thank you. I love you.'

If there is something that you are having difficulty getting
beyond, hold this phrase in your mind, say it to yourself and
direct it at whatever it is you're having difficulty with.

· · · · · ·

'I HAVE NOT FAILED. I HAVE FOUND TEN THOUSAND WAYS THAT DIDN'T WORK.'

· · · · · ·

*Thomas Edison, before finding the right metal to use
for the light filament in the electric light bulb.*

UNIT 7

• • • • • •

- **The Science Bit:** The parietal cortex
- **Mindful Moment:** One on one
- **Motto:** 'When you change the way you look at things, the things you look at change.'
- **EQ Competence:** Focus
- **Power Tool:** DWDWD – Do What you are Doing When you are Doing it
- **Skill Set for Health:** Coming to your senses
- **Homework:** A meal to remember

••••••

You're late!

A lot of mindfulness talk focuses on being present, seeing things as they are, distinguishing 'reality' from our interpretation of it. Sure, it's very powerful when you get that you are not your thoughts and you develop the ability to listen to your chattering monkeys and choose whether to buy into their conversation or not.

Being present is great, but we're always late. The time it takes for us to process and put together the meaning of the input for any event means that it is always already over by the time we are conscious of what happened. This 'reality gap' is about 0.2 seconds, which is a really long time in the life of a neuron.

What's more, we are always comparing incoming signals with a previously constructed 'internal model'. This makes it easier for us to make sense of the multitudinous jumble of input messages we are constantly being bombarded by. We are constantly making it up. We see what we want to see based on this internal model.

Ho-hum!

Other parts of your body may actually register incoming

information faster than your brain – your heart, for example. Your heart has nerve cells, produces neurotransmitters like oxytocin and sends messages to the brain before the brain has put its own story together. This is shocking information to 'head supremacists'! As more and more research emerges around this area, it may be that science itself is bringing about the demise of the so-called 'Age of Reason'.

And ...

As we clean the windscreen through which we view the world, we can get better at noticing the process involved in the way we construct our version of reality. This is different for every single person. Common factors arise by agreement, sure. For example, we can all agree that 'This is a book.' Few would argue with that. But we each have a unique world map, and not realizing this leads to a lot of misunderstandings.

I say 'Let's do dinner.' You hear 'Let's go on a date! Woo-hoo!' I write 'I'd like to discuss that work contract.' You read 'I'm in with a chance!'

······

THE PERSON ACROSS THE TABLE FROM YOU IS NOT EXPERIENCING THE WORLD THE WAY YOU ARE.

······

Knowing that this is going on makes it more likely you will make the effort to find out what the place from which they view it all is actually like, rather than assume it's the same as yours.

In the process of getting better at connecting with the other nervous systems you have in your heart and gut, somatic awareness is key. Being embodied is central to being an integrated fully functioning coherent human being.

EQ Competence: Focus

The final EQ Competence is focus. As self-aware, emotionally intelligent people, we can keep our focus where we want it. We shift it when needed, notice when we lose it, and regain balance, approaching situations rather than avoiding them (see Unit 6). Thoughts gets less sticky. With good somatic awareness, we can notice what's happening on the inside of us, maintaining connection to a strong inner core. With our situational sensitivity and non-verbal intuition, we can bounce back while keeping a clear, open field of view, in touch with what is happening around us.

Our Daily Formal Practice helps us clean the windscreen of our perceptual fields and register change more accurately and more quickly. Sensations, feelings and thoughts are events that come and go, and actions are events that we choose.

How many times have you found yourself reading a book, except that you're not? Your eyes are gazing in the right direction. You might even start to turn the page, only to realize that you've taken in nothing of what was written. Where were you? Lost in thought, going through the motions. How many times have you sat in a meeting appearing to listen, even nodding your head appropriately, but actually miles away?

A young man on the bus the other day, talking to a workmate it seems, said, 'Since I got that email from her, I haven't been able to concentrate. In that meeting I was all over the place. I can't get what she said out of my head. I'm so upset.'

With the Mindful Moments and Daily Formal Practice we are training our brains so we can drag ourselves out of these mental–emotional quagmires and focus where we want. We get better at dropping ruminative thinking, bringing ourselves out of the daydream, and better at recovering our emotional equilibrium.

And it's emotional upset that has the most powerful impact on our ability to focus. Once we are upset, our old friend the amygdala is running the show again and we lose our adaptability, get tunnel vision and locked-in hearing, and our thoughts run on cyclical train tracks.

......

EACH TIME WE SIT, WE ARE NOTICING OUR THOUGHT TRAINS, WITH THOSE CHATTERING MONKEYS ON BOARD, AND INTENTIONALLY BRINGING THE FOCUS OF OUR ATTENTION BACK TO THE BREATH. BUT, LIKE ANY SKILL, IT TAKES PRACTICE.

......

My mum, a wondrous Yorkshire lass, used to say, 'There's none so deaf as them that don't want to hear.' Anyone with children will know this. But what about us? What are *we* screening out? How are we steering our attention in the direction of what we want to hear and see? What are we missing? Are we filtering out information that doesn't fit in with our worldview? Are we subliminally seeing people the way we think they are, based on the past, on the internal model we have built of them, rather than the way they actually are?

What would happen if we were able to notice our interpretation, our unconscious bias, and approach others from a place of openness and curiosity, allowing ourselves to be vulnerable and not know what is going to happen next? Might this allow the other person to show up as who they are, and, in that space, might genuine connection and communication be established?

167

How is your focus? Do you find it difficult to concentrate in a noisy environment? Do you find yourself jumping all over the place from one line of thinking to another, as they collide and spark off new trains of thought? When you first started your Daily Formal Practice were you surprised by the level of noise going on in your head? You have low focus.

Can you stay on track with what you are doing and get back to it when interrupted? Can you juggle several activities without feeling tense as you try to hold on to all the threads simultaneously without getting tangled? Do you block out everything around you to stay focused, and 'fiddle while Rome burns'? Do the people in your life have to poke you to get your attention? You have very high focus.

Describe your focus here:

MY FOCUS

The science bit

Sensory input goes first to the thalamus, a kind of relay station, from which signals get distributed according to source, state and sort code. Most input from our five senses – touch, sight, sound, smell and taste – goes to the parietal lobe, which is a bit like the Clapham Junction of sensory input. Rich connections with the prefrontal cortex determine how much attention gets put on which signals.

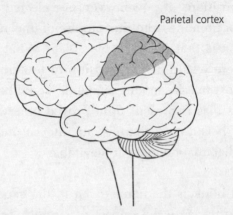

Parietal cortex

We can turn up and dial down the signals we want to attend to. At a cocktail party, we can tune in to one voice, or keep an open scan on the background noise if we are awaiting the arrival of a particular person. A mother will easily pick out her baby's cry from noisy surroundings.

Our intention determines where we put our attention. We dial up and dial down sensory channels accordingly. Emotional upset can hijack this process and skew our attention quite substantially. We hear and see what we want to hear and see to fit in with our worldview. It happens automatically. The policeman who is feeling threatened and in 'amygdala hijack' survival mode will process sensory input according to his or her internal model and can exhibit significant unconscious bias in how they interpret reality.

Selection committees can unwittingly not even consider whole categories of candidates on the basis on implicit bias. People in positions of power, even our elected representatives, are not immune from the impulse of unconscious bias. The paradox is that it's invisible. 'Bias? What bias?' If it weren't, there would be the possibility to address it. Perhaps the most failsafe modus operandi would be to assume unconscious bias is present until proved otherwise, and to seek it out. It is always there – our internal model, filters, beliefs and habituation make it inevitable.

Attentional blink is the name given to the experiment scientist use to measure the impact of emotion on attention. A series of letters are flashed up on a screen. The subject is instructed to push a button every time they notice a certain number appears in the sequence. Easy. Except once the subject has pushed the button they get a rush of excitement. 'Yay, Whoopee! I noticed it!' And their attention blinks so they miss the next number that flashes up soon after the first.

People who meditate regularly demonstrate less attentional blink. They stay calmer, don't have the same level of emotional reaction, and hold their focus on the task in hand better. Imagine how important this is in all the delicate and dangerous processes where human error can have far-reaching consequences – anything that involves quality control, the administration of medication, airport screening, car manufacturing, being in charge of potentially lethal machinery – a car, for instance, or a gun.

Ground control to Major Tom

Have you ever been in a conversation and wondered whether the other person was listening? Or even if they were on the same planet? A lot of us are pretty distracted a lot of the time. Or have you found yourself unable to listen because something someone said triggered you? 'What? They like Daft Punk? Ugh!' Or, in a more serious vein, they say, 'This report needs rewriting', and your head immediately heads for the panic room!

In everyday life, better focus means that when things go a bit pear-shaped around you or you get triggered emotionally, you are more able to bounce back, notice the small signs and deal with the situation appropriately and effectively. That's better EQ.

Think what this means in terms of interpersonal communication. Person A can listen and hear with greater accuracy

Motto:

`IF YOU CHANGE
THE WAY YOU LOOK
AT THINGS, THE
THINGS YOU LOOK
AT CHANGE.´

Wayne Dyer

what Person B is saying. They can read, interpret and translate the micro-expressions and cues that signal Person B's shifting emotional landscape (non-verbal intuition), and pick up the subtext and adjust accordingly (situational sensitivity).

All this leads to greater rapport, empathy and co-operation. Feeling heard and respected, Person B is calmer, more present and more likely to be able to say what they really want to say. Greater transparency, openness and trust are fostered in an upwards spiral of presence. That's good for people and good for business, and essential for mental wellbeing.

Flow

The interesting thing is that when we are doing something that we love, we are naturally focused. We are living in the moment. The self-critical chatter is at a minimum. We find ourselves almost instinctively knowing what to do next. Everything proceeds with a sense of ease, exploration and enjoyment. We are in flow. Brain waves have slowed down, and a variety of functional areas and body systems synchronize, minimizing energy usage. We are present. Our systems are in coherence, which, as we saw earlier, amplifies power.

This is what occurs when a tennis player leaps gazelle-like across the court and hits a winning shot from between his legs. When a rock climber dangles from one hand, trusting her body-mind to do what needs to be done next without interference from her rational mind. When a musician becomes so connected to the music that his instrument seems like an extension of his body ...

Where and when do you feel like this? Recall the story you wrote about as homework in Unit 1. What are you doing when you are in flow, focused, effective, energized and lovin' it?

YOUR FLOW

Mindful Moment: One on one

The Mindful Moment for this unit is 'One on One'. Take one minute once an hour to connect with your body and your senses. Set a timer on your phone to remind you. If you're at work, nobody need know you are doing it.

Take a moment to adjust your posture, pull up through your spine and release your shoulder and jaw. Improve your physiological state by taking a deep breath in and exhaling slowly. Keep breathing more slowly and deeply than usual throughout the one minute. Now dial up your sense of hearing. Stay with that for 15 seconds or so. Now tune in to your nose and notice what you can smell. Then dial up your sense of touch via your body. What can you feel where in your body right now? Finally, connect with something that evokes a sense of appreciation or care in you. Breathe this feeling in through you whole body. Job done.

With all these Mindful Moments, bear in mind that, every time you do them, you are altering your nervous system, retraining your body's nervous system to a neutral and coherent state. After a while this new core balance state becomes the new normal. In addition, you are exercising your LPFC, that CEO function brain area that is the seat of higher functions. You are incrementally upgrading your own systems.

Skill Set for Health: Coming to your senses

The Skill Set for Health theme for this unit is 'Coming to Your Senses'.

'Lost in thought' is not a particularly pleasant place to be. We miss so much of what is going on around us. When head-led, we are mostly operating in Small Self mode. And all those chattering monkeys can drive us mad.

By intentionally dialling up the focus of awareness in our senses, we drive ourselves sane and enrich our experience of life.

What does the door handle feel like in your hand? How does the key sound in the lock? What smells hit you as you open the door? What is your felt sense of who is home and what might be going on there? As you walk in, what do your senses tell you?

Take your time. Switch between senses. Dial them up one by one intentionally. We tend to be visually dominated. What about smell, taste, sound and touch, and that other inexplicable sense of knowing what's going on around us? 'You could cut the atmosphere with a knife.' 'I knew as soon as he walked in the office what had been going on.' Notice your own internal world – the sense of interoception.

Start to listen to these other vital sources of information. Ground yourself in the here and now. What are your senses telling you? Be curious. Be open. Listen to your other brains in your gut and heart.

Practise eating with greater presence. Choose a small item of food that has neither strongly negative nor positive associations for you. In traditional mindfulness courses, the humble raisin is often the foodstuff of choice. Once you have chosen your food item, go to your meditation spot and prepare yourself in the usual way with the three Ps: Place, Posture, Poise.

Take a minute or two to bring your physiological state into balance by focusing on your breath, slowing and deepening your breath in a way that feels comfortable for you. Now, hold your food item in your hands and dial up the sense of touch. Explore it fully with your sense of touch so that you are familiar with every facet of its surface, every texture, and what that feels like. Now dial up your sense of smell. Explore its odours fully.

Look at your item with fresh eyes. Note the colours, the nuances of shade, the way the light catches it. Move it around, so you can explore every aspect of its appearance. When you are ready, bring the item towards your mouth, noticing the sensations in your mouth as you do so. Once the foodstuff is in your mouth, be curious about the feelings that arise, the sensations of texture and taste, the chewing motion, your tongue, the food item's voyage around the cavern of your mouth. Once swallowed, imagine its voyage as it moves down into your body. What lingers in your mouth and senses? Spend a moment to reflect on the food item's journey from creation to your mouth. Finally, express your thanks. Focusing again on your breathing, let the experience of eating something with complete attention sink into your memory bank.

As we discussed in Unit 3, the ability to sense what's going on inside your body, interoception, is an important part of improving your ability to master your emotions. What are you sensing inside your body right now? What is your interoception telling you about how you are feeling?

Power Tool: DWDWD – Do What you are Doing When you are Doing it.

The final Power Tool is DWDWD – Do What you are Doing When you are Doing it. Pay attention to what you are engaged in right now. Engage fully with that.

Do
What you're
Doing
When you're
Doing it.

Start with the sentence 'Right now, I'm ...'. Fill in the blank.

- 'Right now. I'm chopping an onion.'
- 'Right now, I'm thinking about my dentist's appointment.'
- 'Right now, I'm driving the car.'
- 'Right now, I'm noticing feelings of happiness.'
- 'Right now, I'm walking down the stairs.'

Sensations, feelings, thoughts, actions – the substrate of human life. What is going on right now in these four domains?

Bring yourself back to the present. Get curious about what is happening in your experience right now. Even those tasks that you've done a million times over. In fact, *particularly* those ones! Like stashing the dishwasher or washing the dishes. What are you actually doing as you do that? What is that like when you open up all your senses and do what you're doing when you're doing it?

We start to notice the ordinary events in our life in a new way. We see how stunning the rings and patterns and colours of the onion are. We are aware of the smells arising from the freshly washed clothes as we hang it out on the washing line, or from the pavement on our walk to the station. We hear how the sound the kettle makes changes as it starts to boil and how the water sounds as we pour it in our cup. We notice how we can tell if the water coming out of the tap is hot or not.

These little moments of presence add up to a greater

sense of fulfilment and appreciation for life. Focused attention is like a laser beam of effectiveness. The brain wakes up and becomes more coherent. More BDNF, the chemical that promotes new neural connections, is produced. That laser beam cuts through the fog of mental clutter and wandering thought, saving you energy, integrating functioning and synchronizing the many online brain areas involved in what you are doing.

Homework: A meal to remember

The homework for this unit is to prepare and eat one meal with full attention and with all your senses. Practise by having the intention to eat one thing slowly and with all your senses every day.

UNIT 8

••••••

- **The Science Bit:** The healthy brain
- **Mindful Moment:** Your USP
- **Motto:** 'Wear the cloak of life lightly.'
- **Power Tool:** DGDG – Doing Good Does you Good.
- **Skill Set for Health:** Ikagai
- **Homework:** Simplicity

> ......
> `WE MUST NOT CEASE FROM EXPLORATION
> AND THE END OF ALL OUR EXPLORING WILL
> BE TO ARRIVE WHERE WE BEGAN AND TO
> KNOW THE PLACE FOR THE FIRST TIME.´
> ......

T. S. Eliot

Back to the future

Mindful presence is like butter. Fry an egg in butter and it's tastier and less likely to stick to the pan. Spread it on bread and it enhances the lusciousness of your sandwich. Melt it over new potatoes and it enriches taste, aroma and texture to what could otherwise be a rather bland vegetable. Glaze your pastry and it becomes glossy and golden. Butter makes everything a bit better.

Being more present brings the same richness to the experience of our daily lives. It doesn't alter the substrate but shifts the way we relate to it. In its origins, mindfulness was only part of a palette of possibilities designed to help us fulfil our potential. And without this backdrop of wisdom and guidance about how to live a life of integrity and authenticity, its meaning and power are diluted. We end up with a technique, a quick fix for modern-day ailments, a 'thing', hijacked by a twentieth-century medical model that sees us as 'broken' and in need of 'fixing'.

Who we are, our spirit, soul, inner self, whatever you choose to call it, cannot be broken and does not need fixing. It just needs room to breathe, expand its wings and fly.

. . . . . .

'I HAVE GOTTEN RID OF THAT IGNORANT FIST THAT WAS PINCHING AND TWISTING MY SECRET SELF.'

. . . . . .

Rumi

As we clear the windscreen of our perception and come closer to that experience of our own wholeness we are coming back to the beginning, to being who we already always were. Even if life has rubbed the shine off our aspirations, we can regain our excitement about what is possible. Rather than trying to become something, we are getting back in touch with who we always have been. It's like coming home. We are *un*becoming all the patterns, habits, beliefs and attitudes that got in the way.

......

'THERE IS A CRACK [...] IN EVERYTHING. THAT'S HOW THE LIGHT GETS IN.'

......

Leonard Cohen

Sometimes this unbecoming can be uncomfortable. As we shed the skin of our old habitual self, to allow the new truer self to emerge, huge existential questions can arise. This can give rise to inner pain. In today's world, with few roadmaps to guide us through these vital period of transition, our suffering can be labelled as mental illness. Rather than being given guidance in how to shed our skin and unfold our wings anew, there is a risk that we are stigmatized, discriminated against and categorized. Fear can arise in those who hesitate to ask deeper questions about being human, society, what it all means – the fear that, if we pierce the fabric of our consensual reality, it may collapse.

......

'I AM MADE WHOLE BY MY SCARS.'

......

Samuel Menashe

However, such periods of transition are most often seen ret rospectively as the part of our journey that made us whole. As we cracked open the old skin, we regained our self underneath and discovered that it had always been there. That core experience, that fundamental sense of being connected, belonging, being loved and loving, re-emerges.

......

'EMANCIPATE YOURSELF FROM MENTAL SLAVERY. NONE BUT OURSELVES CAN FREE OUR MINDS.'

......

Bob Marley

Shifting the zeitgeist

The Zeitgeist is shifting. The twentieth century was dominated by the perspective of psychological interpretation. The 'unconscious' was seen as a force of darkness, a 'recent discovery' attributed to Freud to explain where we had gone wrong. In fact, Eastern philosophies had been providing understandings and roadmaps for negotiating human consciousness for centuries.

Then came the waves of the West Coast self-help personal development movement to help us get to grips with our murky depths. All well and good. Thousands of self-help books, courses and gurus promised us peace of mind. This encouraged a very individualized view of growth and improvement. It encouraged us to struggle on, to borrow Susan Pivers's term, the 'treadmill of self-improvement.' 'Once I fix myself up,' we told ourselves, 'and untangle all these knots I've got inside me, then I'll be OK.'

More recently, positive psychology has aimed to shift the perspective from what is wrong with us to what is good within us. This is more in keeping with the origins of mindfulness. In its origin, suffering is seen as part and parcel of the human condition. Our journey in this lifetime is to come to know the source of our unnecessary suffering – our mind – and to realize that we are not our mind, to become familiar with its nature, and to live in ways that respect the wholeness and connectedness of life. As we ourselves come closer to our true nature, we realize this connectedness and wholeness. In this state of being, healing, compassion and love become natural expressions of who we are.

Research in the field of neuroscience has shifted the way we see the brain, opening up the possibility that we can release ourselves from our past wiring, and from the boxes imposed on us by labels, concepts, diagnoses and the effects of past events. We all have immense power to learn, grow, shed old selves and mould new ones.

·······

'HAMM: WE'RE NOT BEGINNING TO...
TO... MEAN SOMETHING?
CLOV: MEAN SOMETHING? YOU AND I, MEAN
SOMETHING! AH, THAT'S A GOOD ONE!'

·······

Samuel Becket, *Endgame*

187

What if the notion that we are broken and need fixing was just a belief system generated by, and maintaining, the Zeitgeist that gave birth to it? What if all the 'What is wrong with me?', 'Why?' and 'How do I fix myself?' stuff was in itself part of the problem? In other cultures, both now and in the past, such notions are, and were, regarded as rather odd, if not self-absorbed and misdirected.

Self-esteem, for example, is not a real thing. It's a culturally determined construct. A person from a part the world where they highly value humility, selflessness and social cohesion above personal gain would be judged by Western psychological tests as introverted, lacking in self-confidence and self-worth. This gives us some insight into how culturally dependent our worldview is. The word 'self' crops up a lot here too, being used in the sense of 'I' as a separate entity.

What if more powerful concepts were those of choice and connectedness? What if in this moment now, aware of my past conditioning and in acceptance of it, I could connect with my intention and choose? What if who I am, who I show up in the world as, is the outcome of a series of these choices strung together? How can I be more connected to this creative power?

······

LIFE LIVED CONSCIOUSLY IS A CONTINUOUSLY CREATIVE ACT.

······

We write our own history with each choice. Where we are now is the result of the choices we've made until now. Where we will be in the future is determined by the choices we make today. By being more awake, more intentional, more conscious of our choices, we are writing our own future.

What if the twenty-first century was best served by people who asked themselves the question: 'How can I best contribute my natural strengths, abilities and aptitudes to the world?' What if connecting with a higher sense of purpose, defining our core values and determining to live our lives with integrity in tune with that purpose and those values was the most powerful way to bring wellbeing and fulfilment not just to ourselves but to those around us and in the world at large?

What if we each consciously and intentionally resolved to shift the cult of individualism to a culture of connectedness?

• • • • • •

'YOU NEVER CHANGE THINGS BY FIGHTING THE EXISTING REALITY. TO CHANGE SOMETHING BUILD A NEW MODEL THAT MAKES THE OLD ONE OBSOLETE.'

• • • • • •

Buckminster Fuller

Innies and outies

Are you an innie or an outie? On my journey to recovery and full health, I've found that the more outward facing I am, the better I feel. The more I turned my gaze inwards on my Small Self, examining all the warts and wrinkles, the bigger they got.

When I put my attention on helping the old man off the bus, making eye contact with the bored cashier at the checkout, engaging with genuine interest in dialogue with people, the better I felt about myself, and the more 'I' as Expanded Self showed up. This was – and is – enormously healing. Maybe the best way to find ourselves is by connecting meaningfully with other people.

What we focus on gets bigger. Energy flows where attention goes. It takes consciousness and intention to transform the almost gravitational pull of 'bad stuff'. By turning our gaze outwards to the needs of others, we are catalysing this transformation and our relationship to ourselves.

Some of the most awake and generous people I have worked with are those who, having been given a diagnosis of cancer, give up the battle of becoming and resolved to live more fully now. They get off the self-improvement treadmill and resolve to make the most of who they already are. They give up the struggle for perfection and live in a space of acceptance and gratitude. They give up the obsession with self-fixing and resolve to live fully with what they have.

As one patient said to me: 'I wish everyone could get cancer for a week. Just to wake up and smell the roses. And let go of all the struggle.'

••••••

'THERE ARE TWO WAYS TO LIVE YOUR LIFE.
ONE AS IF NOTHING IS A MIRACLE. THE
OTHER AS IF EVERYTHING IS A MIRACLE.'

••••••

Albert Einstein

Power Tool: DGDG – Doing Good Does you Good

The natural state of the mind is one of equanimity and openness. The natural expression of our being human is through kindness, creativity and connectedness. In stillness, we connect with who we are. In connection, we enhance our sense of who we are. In action, we reveal who we are. In practice, we refine how we express who we are.

••••••

'PRACTISE KINDNESS ALL DAY TO EVERYBODY AND
YOU WILL REALIZE YOU'RE ALREADY IN HEAVEN NOW.'

••••••

Jack Kerouac

All the Skill Set for Health themes encourage an outward gaze, an 'approach' attitude to life, fostering a sense of wholeness and connectedness and thereby building our own fulfilment and wellbeing.

Generous people live longer. Appreciation is one of the most powerful positive emotions there is, bringing with it a shift in our physiological state from fear to safety and trust. Acceptance is the essential prerequisite for growth and fulfilment. Curiosity fires up the brain to facilitate the neurological rewiring that accompanies this growth. Learning points us towards the future with a sense of energy and enthusiasm. Forgiveness frees us up from the past. Coming to our senses enhances embodied presence.

Whenever you feel that you're getting stuck in your Small Self, bogged down in a mind trap, out of touch, locked up in a relationship row, hating the idea of work on Monday, go back to your Resource Kit. Choose one of the Skill Set for Health themes and commit to living it wholeheartedly for a week – or even just for a day. See it as an experiment. I welcome your feedback.

Motto:

∙ ∙ ∙ ∙ ∙ ∙

'WEAR THE CLOAK OF
LIFE LIGHTLY.'

∙ ∙ ∙ ∙ ∙ ∙

Neil Gumenick

The science bit: The healthy brain

Like any other organ of the body, the brain has certain basic requirements to work well, requirements that we, as custodians of this magnificent body part, would do well to cater for.

- **Oxygen:** Breathe deeply enough and regularly enough to get a good exchange of oxygen in and waste gases out. Aerobic exercise will help improve heart health and boost circulation of well-oxygenated blood to your brain tissues.

- **Glucose:** Your brain is particularly sensitive to fluctuations in blood sugar levels, needing a steady level of glucose to work optimally. Make sure that you put fuel in your engine in an intelligent, sustainable way. Avoid quick fix sugary substances when you feel an energy slump and go for protein and natural foodstuffs wherever possible. When your blood sugar drops, the brain interprets this as a threatening situation and releases adrenaline and cortisol to increase blood glucose temporarily. Then it swings in the opposite direction and you crave sugar again. Mood follows along on the sugar roller coaster. A low mood can sometimes be fixed immediately by eating a nutritious sandwich.

- **Hydration:** A decrease of even 1–2 per cent in your hydration levels below optimum will have an impact on your cognitive abilities, such as memory, decision making and focus. Make sure that you drink 500 millilitres of water per 13 kilograms of body weight. That's one pint per 28 pounds. Caffeine, alcohol, illness and exercise will increase your hydration needs. Avoid caffeine-based drinks as they artificially induce the state of adrenaline-driven emergency in your body that we have seen earlier is so damaging.

- **Adrenaline:** Not only does regular exercise bring more oxygen to the brain, it boosts production of chemicals like serotonin that improve mood. There are also gains to be made in heart function, physical fitness, sleep and self-esteem. A caveat to this is that overambitious adrenaline junkies can actually become addicted to exercise. A sensible, sustainable, balanced approach works best.

- **Sleep:** While some busy people wear their sleeplessness as a badge of honour, nothing could be more damaging to your emotional balance, physical energy and mental clarity. IQ drops five points or more after a sleepless night. Six to eight hours' restful sleep is essential for the brain to function well. Just as at night cleaners work their way diligently through offices and the other working spaces of the daytime world, so the brain needs this time to process the waste by-products and toxins of the day's activities. There is even evidence that lack of sleep leads to the accumulation of beta amyloid, the stuff that gums up the synapses in Alzheimer's.

- **Learning:** Keep learning. Seek out opportunities to use your brain creatively and constructively. Most of the decline that occurs with age is due to lack of use. Just as your bulging biceps will fade away once you stop lifting those weights, so it is with the intellect. Avoid boredom. When we are excited, engaged, alert, doing things we love, BDNF (Brain-Derived Neurogenic Factor) is produced, which promotes the development and fusing of new neural pathways. Stay curious with an open mind and your brain will thank you with better functioning.

Skill Set for Health: Ikagai

The Skill Set for Health theme of this final unit is ikagai. This is a Japanese word that has no direct translation into English. That is in itself interesting, as words create worlds. Loosely translated it means 'reason for being', the sense of being connected to something deeper and more meaningful than day-to-day survival, a quality that brings richness and fulfilment to our lives.

For many of us, 'purpose' or 'our life's purpose' is something that we search for. 'What is the purpose of my life?' We look for it 'out there' as if it were a thing.

In Daoist philosophy, the words *tian ming* mean 'mandate from heaven'. In that cosmology, everyone has been given a mandate from heaven, their *tian ming*, their destiny. The job during this lifetime is to fulfil this inner mandate.

The way to fulfil our *tian ming* is to trust deeply in our authentic self, to use the strengths and aptitudes we were given to the best of our ability, and in the service of something bigger than our own needs and desires.

The homework for Unit 1 was to write your 'In the flow' story, a time when you felt energized, alive, effortlessly focused, to identify what your natural strengths and aptitudes are, what you are designed to do, and what you are revitalized by doing. Life works best when we follow our own unique design, our *dao*, if you like.

······

DON'T WASTL THE PERSON YOU ARE LIVING SOMEONE ELSE'S LIFE.

······

Nowadays, people have a bit of a problem with this kind of thinking. We are fed a belief diet emphasizing the need for autonomy, meritocracy, individualism and self-determinism. At the same time, isolation is a major cause of ill health.

Businesses large and small are paying huge sums of money to consultants to try to foster employee enthusiasm and engagement. Lack of connectivity across intra- and inter-cultural divides is huge. People are more lost than ever, as evidenced by the huge rise in mental illness.

The answer lies within, and is there all the time.

·······

'WHAT LIES BEHIND US AND WHAT LIES BEFORE US ARE TINY MATTERS COMPARED TO WHAT LIES WITHIN US.'

·······

Ralph Waldo Emerson

Ikagai helps us connect to this treasure chest within. Create an ikagai for each day, one day at a time.

Before you get out of bed in the morning, take a few moments to focus on the area of your chest around your heart. Imagine your breath is flowing into and out of your heart or chest area, breathing a little slower and deeper than usual. Do this for about a minute. Now ask yourself: 'What is my ikagai for today?' Allow the answer to emerge naturally. Write it down somewhere prominent. As you go about your day, keep coming back to your ikagai and see how you are doing? Renew your intention consciously at every opportunity.

MY IKAGAI

In other words, from a place of being in touch with who you are, create a reason for being in the world today that is bigger than your own personal survival. You make it up. It's an ontological process.

Rather than looking to find ourselves, we are creating who we want to be. We are putting the track down in front of the train as we go along, in tune with our own sense of authentic self and with integrity. This is powerful. This is choice. This is freedom.

Homework: Simplicity

The homework for this unit is simplicity. Many people find that, as they pursue the principles outlined in this book, they automatically start to tidy up the messy areas of their lives. And that includes habits that no longer serve them, like eating biscuits when angry, or watching box sets when tired and then staying up too late. Friendships that are one-sided, where there is more give than take, or a power imbalance that makes one party feel smaller than the other. Jobs that don't fit and make them ill. Situations at work where contagious stress reactions predominate or where gossip builds hostility. Emotional reactions that drain them of energy, such as harbouring resentment, blaming and complaining.

······

'THE HARDEST THING IN THE WORLD IS SIMPLICITY.'

······

James Baldwin

Simplify all the aspects of your life. As you clear out the clutter in your emotional and mental basements and cupboards, do the same in your physical environment. In fact, the two go hand in hand.

Start today. One drawer at a time. The diploma for the MMM course on which this book is based comes in the shape of a large black rubbish bag tied up with a red ribbon in a bow. Clear out everything you don't want or need or absolutely love. Have three piles as you clear stuff out: 'Get rid', 'Keep' and 'Not sure'. Then go through the 'Not sure' again and be honest. Resolve to get every item on to the 'Get rid' or 'Keep' pile.

Now go through the 'Keep' pile again. You'll probably notice that your perception has changed and half of that can go on the 'Get rid' pile now.

Now that you have in your life only those things that you want, love or need, organize the physical world around you to work alongside them. 'A place for everything and everything in its place,' as my mum used to say. Put things in places that make sense to support a simplified, clearer, purposeful life.

More than anything, resolve to bring integrity and clarity to all your dealings with other people. Say what you mean and mean what you say. Don't say you will do something unless you know you will. Say 'no' when you need to. Be truthful in your words and actions.

In a difficult conversation, connect with your heart and your head before you connect your tongue. This Sufi adage is quite useful as a filter before you speak:

......

'IS IT TRUE? IS IT KIND? IS IT NECESSARY? IS IT TIMELY?'

......

Use the Power Tools and the Mindful Moments in your Resource Kit.

The more you practise, the stronger the muscle gets. Soon you'll find that the balance point has shifted. Being centred and grounded is the norm. You have retrained your nervous system to a new normal. All systems upgrade.

Mindful Moment: Your USP

All the Mindful Moments and Power Tools are ways to be more present as you go about your daily life. Get into the habit of using them often. Take one of them and focus on that one consciously for a whole day. Every moment is an opportunity to flex the muscle of presence.

HERE'S A FINAL MINDFUL MOMENT FOR YOU.
What is your USP? What makes you special and unique? What shows up when you walk in the room? It can be difficult to see these things about ourselves. It's as if they were written on yellow stickies stuck on your forehead and you have to guess what is written on them.

In the context of this book, how about borrowing one to start with? How about making your USP your Unlimited Serenity Potential?

U   Unlimited
S   Serenity
P   Potential

Be the one who isn't in a hurry, the one who listens and asks useful questions. The one who lands inside themselves first, then speaks. The one who, by showing up in Expanded Self mode, encourages others to do the same.

This is just suggestion. I'm sure that you can come up with a better USP. It's your choice.

YOUR USP

......

'IT IS NEVER TOO LATE TO BE WHAT YOU MIGHT HAVE BEEN.'

......

George Eliot